Road Warrior Without an Expense Account

Jason Heath

Chicago, Illinois, USA

© 2008 by Jason Heath
All rights reserved.

ISBN 978-0-6152-1365-1

Printed in the United States of America.

Preface: Why Music?

One would have to be crazy to go into music for the money. Dozens of alternate and substantially more financially lucrative career paths immediately spring to mind—medicine, law, web development, programming, engineering, or any other profitable enterprises with great salaries and benefits and ample opportunities for employment exist.

Why pick music?

Music as a profession lacks the financial benefits found in the aforementioned career paths. Even the most desirable positions in the world of music (outside of a rarefied handful of international soloists) typically pay what would be only considered a pedestrian wage in most other skilled professions.
And make no mistake about it. Music (particularly the highly refined subgenres of classical and jazz performance) is a *skilled* profession, with music students frequently obtaining masters or doctoral degrees in their instrument of specialty before embarking on a career.

What awaits these young, intrepid, fresh-faced graduates in today's musical landscape?

This is the question that I shall seek to answer in the following chapters.

Most professional musicians start their careers with the noble goal of creating something beautiful and making a living doing it. Even this seemingly simple goal is surprisingly difficult to achieve, and musicians spend countless hours, days, weeks, months, and years in pursuit of this fleeting and illusory state of being.

The path toward achieving this goal—a living through music—is fraught with peril, and among the greatest pitfalls that befall professional musicians in their early years is the perception of having attained a sustainable career while in reality having been drawn into a vicious and unsustainable cycle.

Road Warrior Without an Expense Account

This basic assumption underlies everything discussed in the following pages. I know that we musicians did not go into this profession for the money, and the purpose of this book is not to complain incessantly about how little we all make but rather to explore situations that allow musicians to be compensated fairly for our work and allowed to earn a living while pursuing our craft. My personal and observational experience, unfortunately, has been that the hidden costs of the freelance life quickly erode any seeming profit from far too many avenues of musical employment.

While the future of established professional musical career paths is uncertain, the tenacity of musicians and their ability to craft new paths for themselves through their imaginative efforts is never in doubt. The method by which musicians will forge new paths in the future and the ability of current educational structures to effectively train the next generation of professional musicians is what we shall explore more deeply in this volume.

While the focus of this book is on the plight of the freelance musician, many of the topics discussed have relevance for all musicians, regardless of their professional specialty. As we shall see, the percentage of professional musicians working predominantly as freelancers rather than tenured employees is increasing with each passing year, and learning what this means for the industry as a whole and how musicians will cope with this evolving landscape is of paramount importance.

Acknowledgements

This book is dedicated to my loving wife Courtney, my supportive parents, and all the wonderful colleagues I've worked with as a professional musician.

Contents

I	Realities of Professional Freelancing	1
II	The Rise and Fall of the Full-Time Orchestra	12
III	Rising Tide, Shrinking Pool	18
IV	Regional Orchestras	23
V	The Vicious Cycle	30
VI	Rats in the Ivory Tower	35
VII	Private Teaching	41
VIII	Burnout	54
IX	Rethinking Music Performance Degrees	62
X	Refocusing (Musical Entrepreneurship)	73

1

Realities of Professional Freelancing

Defining the Role of the Freelance Musician

Most professional musicians do some amount of freelance work, regardless of whether they have a full-time orchestra or university position. New York Philharmonic brass players perform in churches on Sundays, Chicago Symphony musicians play side jobs for contractors, and Cleveland Orchestra musicians teach lessons in a variety of settings. Even these musicians, all members of the most revered and highly compensated ensembles in the United States, regularly engage in what most consider "freelance" employment from time to time. From a certain perspective, all musicians are freelancers—some simply more so than others—and what follows therefore applies to nearly all musicians. This chapter covers some topics that anyone even considering a career in orchestral performance should ponder. While this information is based on experiences within the United States, musicians in other countries may find that it resonates with their experiences as well.

Even simply using the term "professional orchestra musician" can be somewhat misleading, for a freelance musician can easily be considered just as much of a "professional" as any full-time symphonic musician. Despite this fact, the phrase "professional orchestra musician" is used in this book to denote an individual in a full-time, tenure track orchestral position. Most of these positions have certain benefits in common, are members of the International Conference of Symphony and Opera Musicians (ICSOM), and are usually governed by an American Federation of Musicians collective bargaining agreement. All of these factors make the employment experience of a full-time orchestral musician substantially different from that of a professional freelancer, and these differences are what I am attempting to highlight in this analysis.

The majority of mid- to large-sized metropolitan areas (500,000 people or more) in the United States support one fully professional orchestra, with anywhere from 50% to 100% of the musicians in these ensembles retained as full-time employees. While some of the largest metropolitan areas (like New York, Chicago, and San Francisco) may support a full-time opera orchestra as well, for the vast majority of cities these positions are part-time employment, and no cities support two or more full-time orchestras.

Metropolitan areas consisting of fewer than 500,000 people rarely support full-time professional orchestras, though there are a few rare exceptions (like the Naples Philharmonic in Naples, Florida). These mid-sized metropolitan areas often utilize a core of full-time musicians (making up from 15% to 30% of the ensemble membership), augmented by part-time, per-service musicians for the ensemble's larger-scale performances. This membership arrangement allows for a solid musical skeletal structure that is consistent from performance to performance and which is fleshed out by part-time freelancers for larger works. Keeping only a percentage of the orchestra's membership on the full-time payroll allows for a reasonable and sustainable budget for smaller organizations while still providing the consistency provided by a core of full-time professional musicians.

Since most of the musicians in these smaller orchestras are not paid a living wage in their orchestral position, what do these non-salaried musicians do to augment their performance income? These non-core musicians usually receive none of the medical or other benefits of their full-time colleagues, forcing them to find other opportunities to generate a sustainable income and offset these costs. Many freelance musicians also supplement their performance income with private teaching or part-time adjunct university teaching, supplementing the ranks of full-time faculty at local institutions.

While smaller metropolitan areas may have freelancers filling university instrumental faculty positions, in cities with full-time orchestras these university positions are often held by the same players holding the professional orchestra jobs in that city—a good thing for everybody but the freelancers. I believe that these professional orchestra members should hold these university positions. For young instrumentalists interested in a career in orchestral performance, studying with a top-tier orchestral professional is a must. In the world of the double bass, for example, the vast majority of double bassists winning full-time orchestral positions have studied with a professional orchestra player, and the same is true across the board for many instruments. Want a full-time orchestra gig? Then study with someone who has held one of these positions (or has held one at some point in his or her career, at least), not with a freelancer. There are obvious exceptions to this rule, but the current and former professional activities of prospective teachers should certainly factor into the decision-making process of potential students during the application process.

The downside of having professional orchestral players holding these positions for the greater music community is that, of course, it further reduces the job market for freelance musicians. The most desirable (and highest paying) adjunct teaching positions and lecturer positions in instrumental performance end up being held by people with another primary income stream in the professional music world, squeezing even more water out of the metaphorical freelance sponge. As a result, musicians wanting to teach at a university must often find an institution undesirably far away—too distant for any sensible professional orchestral musician. Adjunct university instructors regularly commute 60, 80, 100, or more miles each way (frequently without any mileage compensation) to work at these adjunct university positions.

Road Warrior Without an Expense Account

Surprisingly, even those "undesirable" university positions often end up being held by full-time orchestra professionals. Many professional orchestra musicians also enjoy teaching, seeing it as a complementary activity to their performing career and a way to "give something back" to the world of music. This is a good thing—people should be studying with orchestral professionals if they want a job in an orchestra. On the other hand, each of these positions could have proven to be the cornerstone of a local freelancer's career were it not taken up by the local professional orchestra player.

This pecking order also holds true in the realm of professional freelance opportunities for most metropolitan areas. For example, I can list at least a dozen freelance ensembles in the Chicago metropolitan area (my base of operations) that are made up predominantly of musicians from the Chicago Symphony and the Lyric Opera of Chicago.

Realities of Professional Freelancing

Chicago Symphony
Lyric Opera
University faculty
freelancers

This also is a good thing (despite reducing available opportunities for players like me!). If an ensemble has the opportunity to use players of this top-tier professional caliber, they would be fools not to do so. It is not the responsibility of an arts organization to create balanced employment opportunities throughout the greater musical community; their goal is to secure the services of the best players available for their ensemble. These professional orchestra players are where they are for a reason, and if they want to perform outside of their full-time orchestral job, it is their right to do so.
Personally, I love playing freelance gigs with players from these top-tier professional orchestras, and I know that audiences appreciate

knowing that they are watching "musicians from the Cleveland Orchestra" rather than a group of indistinguishable freelancers. As a result, much of the best freelance orchestral playing is done by these same players with full-time orchestral positions, enriching the musical scene of the metropolitan area. At the same time, these players unintentionally squeeze even more water out of the freelance sponge by performing these freelance jobs.

Is this a raw deal for freelancers? Undoubtedly so, but as previously stated, it is not the responsibility of arts organizations to equally and equitably distribute employment opportunities. The same is true in business, basketball, or any other field of endeavor. Arts organization managers want the best qualified and best performing individuals for their ensembles, and if the best (in this case, the full-time orchestra musicians) want to participate, arts organizations would be fools to turn them away.

Holding full-time orchestral positions gives classical musicians an aura of perceived legitimacy in the eyes of musicians and contractors, making it highly likely that these individuals will be approached first for the best freelance work. Fair or not, this is one of the realities of freelancing, and it is something that one should be aware of when considering a career in orchestral music. An extremely low percentage of music students ever attain a position with a full-time orchestra, and later chapters demonstrate how this situation gets worse with each passing year.

Musicians intent on pursuing a career in orchestral performance need to be prepared for the likely possibility of a freelance rather than tenure-track career, and they need to possess a skill set adequate for dealing with this new reality. A freelancer is not the first pick and simply never will be without being a member of the area's full-time orchestra.
At first glance, musical employment opportunities appear to be everywhere. Symphonic concerts, opera companies, and musical theater productions all employ musicians, and a rough tally of the employ-

Realities of Professional Freelancing

ment opportunities of any mid-to-large urban area can be cause for optimism. When looking more deeply, however, one realizes that a significant number of those ensembles and institutions are populated by musicians from those two major ensembles. In Chicago, for example, the Chicago Symphony and the Lyric Opera of Chicago are both full-time professional ensembles that cross-pollinate across a significant percentage of freelance ensembles, turning up at community centers, regional orchestras, contractor gigs, and university teaching jobs all across the metropolitan area. These musicians are simply taking extra work as their schedule permits, and there is certainly nothing wrong with this—in fact, the entire metropolitan musical and educational community benefits from the presence of these top-tier instrumentalists. Their presence at engagements outside of their primary ensemble does significantly impact the available opportunities for musicians outside of these ensembles, however, and therefore directs the amount of available opportunities for the freelance musician.

When analyzing the classical double bass scene in Chicago, one finds nine full-time double bass positions in the Chicago Symphony and six full-time double bass positions in the Lyric Opera of Chicago. Over the past twenty years, four double bassists have won positions in these ensembles--three in the Chicago Symphony and one in the Lyric Opera of Chicago, averaging out to one full-time double bass position every five years in this metropolitan area. These employment statistics are exponentially worse for instruments like trumpet, harp, or oboe. The only large non-adjunct university position not held by one of these fifteen players (as of this writing in 2008) is the double bass position at Northwestern University.

Let me reiterate this: there is only one non-adjunct university position in this metropolitan area of over nine million that is not held by one of these fifteen full-time orchestral bassists! And even this one position is, at the time of this writing, a lecturer position, not a tenure-track professorship. Think about that statistic before investing tens of thousands of dollars and a decade of your life getting a B.M. , M.M., and D.M. in music performance! If one desires a double bass tenure track position at the university level, don't plan on moving to Chicago anytime soon.

Classical Double Bass Employment Statistics in

Metropolitan Chicago

Size of metropolitan area	9,000,000
Number of full-time double bass positions	15
Positions compared to population	One job per 600,000 people
Average rate of vacancy	One vacancy every five years

Statistically speaking, the odds of becoming mayor of a city like Milwaukee, Wisconsin (population 578,887), are better than the odds of obtaining a full-time double bass position in Chicago!

In addition to those fifteen players, there are a handful of double bassists based in Chicago making a full-time living doing a combination of freelance orchestral playing and university teaching. A couple of these players manage to work predominantly in Chicago and the nearby suburbs. The rest drive long miles across multiple states, balancing three, four, or five regional orchestras, being maxed out on attendance requirements, staying in hotels, or even renting multiple apartments in different cities. There is a definite pecking order for the freelance community as well, and young musicians may have a difficult time initially making any headway in this arena. Regardless of what a musician still in college may think, it is not easy to simply walk into a new community as a freelancer and immediately get quality work. The better the work, the more likely players are to hang on to it. Most beginning freelancers, therefore, will have to drive for their dollars.

If one inserts a push pin on a map in the dead center of any major metropolitan area in the United States and starts to draw concentric circles radiating outward, the farther away one gets from that push pin the worse the gig usually gets—the pay diminishes, the working conditions get shadier, and the quality of the ensemble decreases. Freelancer income decreases exponentially as one radiates outward from the center of the push-pinned metropolitan area until one finally begins to run into the gig circles of another metropolitan area. Pay and conditions tend to go up as one approaches the center of the new metropolitan area, but the odometer on the car keeps ticking, and those hidden freelancer expenses start eroding that paycheck.

Certain high-density geographic regions of the United States exhibit a different set of behaviors than those described earlier. The East Coast urban corridor (including New York City, Philadelphia, and Washington, D.C.), in particular, consists of metropolitan areas with such frequency as to provide a sustained corridor of potential orchestral employment for the freelance musician, with musical and remunerative qualities varying according to local economic factors rather than proximity to any particular metropolitan area. This area of the United States has a particularly rich depth of opportunity for the orchestral freelance musician, with similar traits in evidence (though to a lesser extent) in the greater Los Angeles/San Diego metropolitan area in southern California.

Outside of these few examples, most metropolitan areas in the United States function according to the aforementioned gig circle principle. Every extra 50 miles of distance from the center of a metropolitan area tends to decrease overall compensation by 30-50%, with gigs 100 miles away often paying far less than half of their more advantageously located inner neighbors.

Young musicians focused on a career in orchestral performance need to get some experience performing in orchestras, and the positions that are most available to these young performers tend to be in the furthest reaches of these gig circles. Even these positions can be extremely competitive, but they are significantly more attainable than the work in the closer gig circles. Most freelance musicians seeking to earn a living playing orchestral music must make long commutes in different directions radiating outward from their metropolitan area.

I have been doing this sort of work my entire life. When I lived in Sioux Falls, South Dakota, I regularly commuted to Sioux City, Iowa, to work. Conversely, many musicians came in from places like Minneapolis, Omaha, and other nearby cities to play in the South Dakota Symphony. After graduating from music school, I began working in various orchestras across Wisconsin, Illinois, Indiana, Iowa, and down as far as Memphis, Tennessee (nearly 600 miles south of Chicago). Although this may seem like a wide geographic net to cast for employment, this long-haul regional wandering is the norm rather than the exception for freelancers.

The number of freelance musicians escalates each year as more students graduate from programs of musical study and come to the realization that few professional positions are actually available. When I auditioned for the Elgin Symphony in 2000, only a couple of bass players showed up for the audition. The following audition in 2003 brought out 25 bass players, including many with advanced degrees from major universities and players with significant ICSOM orchestra experience. When the Charleston Symphony (S.C.) held auditions for principal bass in 1999, eleven bassists showed up for the audition. In 2002 they held another audition and 75 bassists showed up.

As more and more players enter the freelance scene nationwide, the competitiveness of these jobs rivals the competitiveness of professional jobs from an earlier generation. These part-time gigs have become the "new jobs" of the current generation of music students. The level of experience and education one needs to land a position in the Elgin Symphony, Canton Symphony, or other such job is now in many cases the same as what a full-time major orchestral position requires. The level of education needed for these jobs (most people landing even part-time freelance orchestra positions have at least a B.M. and usually a M.M.) escalates every year as university tuition continues to skyrocket. What used to put one on the path to a full-time orchestral performance career now may not even get one into a part-time regional orchestra.

The disparity in pay between full-time and part-time orchestras can be huge. While the average 2006 ICSOM salary was $53,549, the average Regional Orchestra Players Association (ROPA) orchestra paid a scant $13,000 per year. Even orchestras with full sets of multi-performance monthly classic and pops concerts often pay section players less than $10,000 per season before taxes. A freelancer interested in a career in orchestral performance must therefore stitch these part-time regional orchestra positions together into a "Frankenstein" career—scary and disturbing, but nevertheless alive.

The Rise and Fall of the Full-Time Orchestra

A Brief History of the "Golden Age" of Symphonic Music

The traditional pot of gold at the end of the rainbow for a student pursuing professional instrumental study at a university is a position in a salaried symphony orchestra. Ever since my early teens, I was constantly encouraged to focus my musical energies on preparing to audition for these salaried symphony orchestras, the attainment of one of these positions being the primary metric of success in the instrumental music performance world. The number of available full-time orchestral positions has been shrinking yearly at a regular rate since the 1980s, however, while the number of students seeking these jobs has grown exponentially. Before dissecting this troubling phenomenon, an overview of 20th century trends in orchestral employment is in order.

The golden age of full-time orchestral employment began with the rapid influx of corporate giving in the late 1960s and began to decline slowly but steadily in the early 1980s. Prior to the 1960s, few of the top tier orchestras paid a living wage. Chicago Symphony musicians

The Rise and Fall of the Full-Time Orchestra

mowed lawns in the summer to pay their bills in the 1940s, and orchestras with a more modest pedigree (like the Milwaukee Symphony) were often volunteer community orchestras. Most performing classical musicians prior to the 1960s would be seen as freelancers today, playing in a wide variety of musical venues and styles on piecemeal wages. Symphonic work made up only a small percentage of the income of classical musicians in the first half of the 20th century. Vaudeville, musical theater, recordings, radio work, jingles, and other such work presented the performing musician with a plethora of options for employment, and symphonic music was definitely not the highest paying activity. The Chicago Union Hall resembled the Chicago Board of Trade in the 1940s and 50s as contractors and musicians bustled about, each vying for the other's services.

The classical music environment began to change drastically in the 1960s with the rise in corporate giving to orchestras. Prior to this point, classical music paid performers with revenue from ticket sales. Musicians ended up working for many concert promoters and impresarios, since no single ensemble was likely to generate sufficient revenue on its own to provide a living wage. Private lessons, recording sessions, and other side work filled out the typical musician's schedule. Corporate giving allowed orchestras, for the first time, to pay out more than their ticket sales generated, enabling many ensembles to put their musicians on salary (along with greatly expanding their administrative staff, building new halls, and engaging in other high-cost activities).

The number of music schools offering performance degrees also mushroomed during this era, as did the number of students entering such programs. Again, there are many contributing factors to this trend, but at least part of the reason for this increase in enrollment and number of programs had to do with the new career paths available to professional musicians. Being an orchestral musician was increasingly seen as a "respectable" career, complete with pension, benefits, and regular hours. The fact that this salary and benefits package was largely funded by corporate giving and not by ticket sales or other such hard transactions did not matter in the minds of most musicians. There were jobs and this next generation of conservatory-trained musicians was well-prepared to acquire them.

19th Century
Impresarios
Corporate giving
Leonard Bernstein
World War II
Full-Time Orchestras

It is interesting to note that, although more people are listening to classical music now than ever before, a strong case can be made that classical music had its widest saturation in the public sphere in the 1950s. Leonard Bernstein's tenure with the New York Philharmonic,

The Rise and Fall of the Full-Time Orchestra

the rise of a stable, prosperous, post-World War II middle-class audience, the rise in popularity of the 33 1/3 LP record, and many other factors contributed to this period as being, if not the only golden age, then certainly one of the golden ages of classical music popularity. This era transpired a good decade-and-a-half before the explosion in corporate giving that precipitated the creation of so many orchestral jobs, and it is worth noting that the popularity of this art form did not coincide with the infusion of cash into the infrastructure delivering this art form.

The jobs created by corporate giving in the late 1960s and early 1970s had both positive and negative consequences for the orchestral world. By 1975 most major (population 1,000,000+) metropolitan areas had a full-time symphony orchestra. These ensembles increasingly offered stable employment opportunities for classical musicians, but they simultaneously created large bureaucratic organizations whose purpose was self-perpetuation and growth. Again, this is not necessarily a negative development, but it represents a distinct shift in the world of classical music dissemination. American classical music in the 19th and early 20th century was based on a commercial need. Impresarios from that era hired musicians for engagements with the sole purpose of making a profit. If the production turned a profit, the impresario would mount another production in a similar vein and continue mining a profit until that stream dried up, at which point he would focus his energies on a new product, perpetuating the cycle of profitable performing.

Contemporary Broadway productions are a great example of this sort of modern-day entrepreneurial musical activity. No one mounts a mammoth musical production like "The Lion King" or "Wicked" as a losing venture. Investors fund these shows to generate a profit, and artistic decisions are made with this goal in mind.

This is not to say that a symphony orchestra should be run like a Broadway production; in fact, running a symphony orchestra with securing the organization's bottom line as the primary concern is likely to create a lowest common denominator product. A lot of the work I do is for modern-day impresarios, and the work itself is often of dubious artistic merit.

The most significant difference between this "golden age" and the latter half of the 20th century is that music was expected to turn a profit and pay for itself with ticket sales. Orchestral opportunities prior to 1960 didn't pay a living wage because, simply put, there wasn't enough money coming into these organizations to warrant such expenditures. Many musicians probably considered these orchestra jobs to be a supplement to a full and busy individualistic freelance career.

As these symphonic institutions grew in stature, they naturally took on more employees to maintain and increase corporate and individual giving. The percentage of budgetary revenue generated from ticket sales shrank as salaries climbed ever higher for musicians. By the latter decades of the 20th century, orchestral administration resembled museums in its structure more than the entrepreneurial one-shot ventures of impresarios of earlier generations.
Symphonic institutions have had differing levels of success depending on region, economy, culture, local corporate and philanthropic entities, and a myriad of other factors. While some have succeeded and some have failed, it is important to note that the number of orchestral playing positions available in these organizations nationwide reached their highest numbers in the late 1970s and have been steadily declining since that time.

Although the population of the United States continues to grow, virtually no new professional orchestras with full-time positions have emerged. The opposite has actually occurred. Each economic recession in the United States knocks off a few professional symphony orchestras. The Savannah, Tulsa, Florida Philharmonic, and San Jose Symphonies are a few victims of the most recent recession. These orchestras are gone—defunct, destroyed, disappeared. Hundreds of full-time orchestra playing positions also evaporated from the United States with the bankruptcy of these organizations, and the likelihood of these institutions remerging and reinstating all of these musicians is dim.

Other orchestras retrench positions as people retire for budgetary reasons. For example, several prominent professional orchestras recently eliminated their full-time harp position after the previous player retired, and many orchestras regularly play "short" in certain string sections (using only 10 instead of 12 cellos, for instance) instead of filling these positions through auditions. This practice of playing "short" can continue for many seasons, with these unfilled positions often being retrenched during a future collective bargaining process.

Rising Tide, Shrinking Pool

*Why More Musicians Are Competing
For Fewer Opportunities*

As the actual number of full-time playing positions decreases with each passing year, the number of music school graduates seeking these positions increases. In fact, there seems to be more interest in obtaining employment with a full-time symphony orchestra than ever before—an especially disturbing trend when coupled with the ever increasing decline in positions available to these players. Approximately 700 new orchestral position candidates enter the audition circuit fresh out of music school each year. A reasonable estimate based on the orchestras that have folded each year would be that there are 10 fewer orchestral positions in the country than there were the year before.

The orchestras that comprise the International Conference of Symphony and Opera Musicians (ICSOM) employ a little over 4000 full-time professional orchestral musicians in the United States and Canada at the present time. The Regional Orchestra Players' Association (ROPA) consists of a combination of per-service and full-time orchestral musicians. Excluding the members of Canadian orchestras but factoring in the full-time positions of the ROPA conference, one can

Rising Tide, Shrinking Pool

assume that there are approximately 4500 full-time orchestral positions in the United States.

The ICSOM conference is comprised of 52 orchestras and is made up predominantly of full-time orchestral positions, while the ROPA conference is comprised of 68 orchestras, with the bulk of the positions being per-service.

How often do these positions open up? Although many factors come into play, each full-time orchestra in the United States typically has a handful of vacancies each season. An analysis of the total full-time positions available in orchestras nationwide results in an average of between 150 and 200 auditions for full-time orchestral positions each season.

Although this may seem at first glance to be a healthy candidate-to-position ratio, many of these positions are filled by players who already hold a position in another full-time orchestra. It is quite common to see players "step up" through the ranks of full-time orchestras, starting with a full-time ROPA orchestra, moving to a moderately sized ICSOM orchestra, and perhaps finally winning a job in a top-ten ICSOM orchestra. The number of positions available to players new to the full-time orchestra system is therefore much lower than this initial figure; around 100 existing positions are filled each season by musicians fresh to the full-time orchestral employment market.

Imagine that no one but these 700 new faces on the audition scene are currently looking for a job during the first year of the following analysis:

Year 1 – 14% probability of audition success
700 candidates auditioning
100 available positions
600 unsuccessful candidates

19

Now year two rolls around. We've still got those 600 candidates who haven't won a job last year. Let's assume that 300 people on the audition circuit quit looking each year. That would still leave 300 candidates from year one—a reasonable (and perhaps overly optimistic) estimate given how many musicians audition for years and years before either quitting or else landing a job.

Year 2 – 10% probability of audition success
700 new candidates + 300 old candidates = 1000 candidates auditioning
1000 candidates auditioning
100 available positions
900 unsuccessful candidates

Those are still good odds, but watch what happens as time progresses. These figures also don't consider any additional increase in music graduate numbers and don't take into account the decline in available positions.

Year 3 – 8% probability of audition success
700 new candidates + 600 old candidates = 1300 candidates auditioning
1300 candidates auditioning
100 available positions
1200 unsuccessful candidates

Rising Tide, Shrinking Pool

Year 4 – 6% probability of audition success
700 new candidates + 900 old candidates = 1600 candidates auditioning
1600 candidates auditioning
100 available positions
1500 unsuccessful candidates

Year 5 – 5% probability of audition success
700 new candidates + 1200 old candidates = 1900 candidates auditioning
1900 candidates auditioning
100 available positions
1800 unsuccessful candidates

Year 6 – 4% probability of audition success
700 new candidates + 1500 old candidates = 2200 candidates auditioning
2200 candidates auditioning
100 available positions
2100 unsuccessful candidates

This pool of unsuccessful applicants continues to grow each year. Here is what things look like after a few more years:

Year 10 – 3% probability of audition success
700 new candidates + 2700 old candidates = 3400 candidates auditioning
3400 candidates auditioning
100 available positions
3300 unsuccessful candidates

At some point it is likely that attrition rates would rise above 300 individuals per year, but there is an increasing tendency for older players to remain active on the audition scene well into middle age. Perhaps the extreme competitiveness of the contemporary audition scene delays the job-winning process for many individuals. Candidates may be in their late 30s or early 40s before winning their first full-time position, if they are able to win one at all! Also, this analysis doesn't take into account any retrenchment of positions or loss of opportunities due to the bankruptcy of orchestras (something that is happening increasingly with each passing year).

Though certainly depressing to the young musician in search of full-time orchestral employment, ruminating on these statistics can glean some valuable lessons. These statistics effectively illustrate the emerging employment outlook for classical musicians. When musicians on the audition circuit can't get full-time orchestral jobs, they often turn to (and have been turning to in increasing numbers) the regional orchestra world to find employment.

The absence of adequate employment for qualified candidates in full-time orchestras propels more top-notch players into the part-time regional orchestra circuit each year, with both positive and negative implications for both orchestra and player.

Regional Orchestras

Benefits and Costs of Working in Multiple Regional Ensembles

What constitutes a regional orchestra? For the purposes of this chapter, regional orchestras will be defined as organizations that employ professional musicians but do not offer a salary and other benefits of full-time employment. The organizational structure is virtually identical to the full-time symphony orchestra and is quite different from the community orchestra. Regional orchestras usually (but not always) have a collective bargaining agreement through the American Federation of Musicians.

The following references to regional orchestras are not limited to member orchestras from the AFM's Regional Orchestra Players Association (ROPA) conference. Although this conference represents a healthy number of regional orchestras nationwide, an ensemble can easily qualify as a regional orchestra according to this definition without a ROPA affiliation. For the purposes of this chapter, if an orchestra pays a salary, it belongs to the full-time orchestra category. If it pays a per-service wage, it is a regional orchestra.

Road Warrior Without an Expense Account

Many non-musicians are not aware of the difference between a community orchestra and a regional orchestra. Differences between these two organizational structures are described in the following pages:

Community Orchestra – Usually comprised of amateur musicians. There is generally either no pay involved or a small honorarium ($15-25 per service) to cover expenses for the musicians. The conductor of such an organization will typically be the only musician compensated. Players may be auditioned or may be picked to play with no audition at all. There is a mutual understanding (or there should be!) that these players are performing in these community orchestras for the love of it and not as a means to a living; and while members strive for high performance standards, there is not necessarily an expectation of a completely polished product. It's like being a good golfer versus being on the PGA Tour. These community orchestras will sometimes hire professional players as principal players or as 'ringers' to fill out the section, and these players will be compensated at a more professional scale. The structure of these organizations is set up with the amateur in mind, with weekly rehearsals, community events, punch and cookies at the breaks, and a general "church social" kind of feeling.

Regional Orchestra – These organizations are comprised of trained professional musicians. The players in this level of orchestra are specialists in their instrument, usually having gone to music school and having demonstrated excellence on their instrument for a long period of time. Think of these orchestras as the minor leagues. There are lots of great players in the minor leagues, and they often move on to the major leagues. The organization of these orchestras usually falls under a collective bargaining agreement, and the bureaucracy of these organizations resembles that of a full-time professional orchestra. These orchestras can pay well per service, but they do not offer full-time employment.

Full-Time Orchestra – These jobs are careers unto themselves, and they have been the traditional employment objective for musicians interested in pursuing an orchestral performance career in the latter half of the 20th century. These organizations provide musicians with a regular salary and benefits.

My Story

At the time of this writing, I am currently a member of the Milwaukee Ballet Orchestra and Elgin Symphony, two regional orchestras included in the American Federation of Musician's Regional Orchestra Players Conference (ROPA). Working in these two organizations has provided me with some insight into the benefits and challenges of regional orchestra employment.

My experience with regional orchestras has been that they often provide the musician with steady employment and good pay for the week--but only for that particular week. The typical regional orchestra plays one concert cycle per month (two in a good month). Orchestras like the Elgin Symphony in Illinois generally play three concerts each performance week, which results in a seven service week, while the Milwaukee Ballet Orchestra in Wisconsin will do four or more performances in a work week.

The compensation for regional orchestras can vary greatly, and it is not always commensurate with the quality of the orchestra. Some regional orchestras pay $375 per week, and some pay $1000 a week or more—it all depends on location, quality of the group, number of services, and other such factors. Playing in a regional orchestra can, for the weeks in which one is employed, closely resemble playing in a full-time orchestra in terms of working conditions, repertoire, and pay, and it can serve as a satisfactory option for musicians looking to pursue a career in orchestral performance.

Road Warrior Without an Expense Account

The problem with this kind of work is that it typically only occurs one week per month for each regional orchestra. Since most individuals or families simply can't pay their bills on one week of work per month, regional orchestra musicians often audition for positions in several different regional orchestras to assemble a patchwork orchestral performance career.

Having a patchwork career has its pluses and minuses. Many people enjoy the variety that comes with playing with different organizations, and they appreciate not having to depend on a single income stream (if you have a full-time orchestra job and it goes belly-up, you're in a tight spot).

It is theoretically possible to hold several different regional orchestra jobs with 10 week seasons each and assemble a 38- to 40-week job out of them. I have come close to achieving this several times in my career. In recent years, I was a member in or played significant portions of the season with the following regional orchestras:

Regional Orchestras

1. Elgin Symphony
2. IRIS Chamber Orchestra
3. Milwaukee Ballet Orchestra
4. Lake Forest Symphony
5. Chicago Opera Theater
6. Chicago Philharmonic
7. Chamber Opera Chicago
8. Chicago Jazz Philharmonic
9. Des Moines Metro Opera
10. Rockford Symphony
11. Illinois Symphony
12. Spoleto USA Festival
13. Racine Symphony
14. Waukesha Symphony
15. Present Music
16. Memphis Symphony
17. Northwest Indiana Symphony
18. Chicago Master Singers
19. Midsummer's Music Festival
20. Music by the Lake
21. L'Opera Piccola

All of these organizations have a regional orchestra set-up in terms of compensation and schedule. I have played with full-time orchestras in metro Chicago like the Lyric Opera of Chicago and community orchestras like the Northbrook Symphony and the Elmhurst Symphony, but these models differ from the regional orchestra model discussed here.

Although I currently hold only two tenured positions in regional orchestras, in any given season I will perform with 8-10 different regional orchestras on a regular or semi-regular basis. The reason I play with so many different groups can be summed up in one word:

Scheduling

Scheduling is the single biggest problem facing freelance musicians playing in regional orchestras. Along with the better working conditions associated with a regional orchestra job comes minimum service requirements. Most regional orchestras have some sort of policy requiring a musician to play anywhere between 50-95% of all offered services. Again, this figure can vary greatly depending on the particular organization, but there is usually some sort of minimum attendance requirement to remain a member of any regional orchestra.
This would not be a problem if regional orchestra schedules didn't constantly conflict with each other. One could hold three or four regional jobs and be working a respectable length season (albeit with no benefits) if the weeks of employment dovetailed with each other. The unfortunate reality is that orchestras tend to book similar weeks. Orchestras don't usually do subscription concerts during Thanksgiving, Easter, and other holiday weeks, and many have a strange tendency to do concerts the very first week of the month. The result is that a musician who is a member of multiple regional orchestras has constant inter-orchestra conflicts.

As an example, let's take a musician who is a member of three regional orchestras. Each of these orchestras has ten subscription weeks of work, which in an ideal world would total 30 weeks of work per season. This idealistic scenario would give the musician approximately eight months of work, which would resemble an ICSOM orchestra that had no summer season. The musician would still typically not have any benefits provided, but 30 weeks of work plus some teaching and other freelance work could easily make for a successful career.

The unfortunate reality is that at least ten of those weeks would conflict with each other, resulting in about 20 weeks of actual employment. Also, the minimum attendance requirements that many regional orchestras maintain begin to cause problems. These conflicting weeks mean that one has to "sub out" of one orchestra in order to play with the other ones, often putting the musician in the precarious position of being perpetually at the maximum number of allowed absences. This 1/3 reduction of work from the ideal three-orchestra schedule not only reduces the musician's income but locks those remaining 20 weeks down, often preventing the musician from taking any of those remaining weeks off for more lucrative subbing opportunities, auditions, and the like.

During my years of simultaneously holding four to five regional orchestra positions, I was constantly in danger of being fired from all four or five of them due to scheduling conflicts. This means that when I get called to substitute in a prestigious orchestra I have to weigh the dangers of being fired from my current tenured positions for the prospect of better, but more irregular (and not guaranteed) work. Holding numerous regional orchestra contracts is essential to guaranteeing a steady income as a freelance classical musician, but it has the adverse effect of stretching musicians across too many ensembles like cream cheese across too many bagels, maxing out their attendance requirements and making it difficult to progress professionally.

5

The Vicious Cycle

Inherent Limitations in Freelance Employment Options

I often wondered, as I entered the classical music freelance world, how one could possibly put together an income in this business. Some "politically smart" auditions I took my last year of graduate school had me (through blind luck more than anything) join the Chicago freelance scene fairly smoothly, allowing me to play with the best groups in the area my first year out of school. Watching my colleagues arrive from their suburban homes in their nice cars, I would wonder how on Earth they managed to make ends meet. After all, we played the same gigs, but I was in debt up to my neck, driving a car with 200,000 miles on it, and barely paying my rent.

How can one survive financially in the freelance business, let alone thrive?

The challenges and limitations of putting together the schedules of various regional orchestras to assemble a career were discussed in previous chapters. Although in theory one could assemble three or four part-time orchestra schedules to create a full-time work load (albeit one without the security and benefits of a full-time position), in reality pervasive scheduling conflicts cause one to stretch absence requirements of contract positions and accept part-time work with 8 to 12 organizations in order to secure a living.

Unfortunately, many freelancers face a fundamental lack of job security and find themselves on a slippery slope toward underemployment over the years. This is a problem that manifests itself quite differently in the world of self-employed music making than it does in the world of business.

In many ways we musicians operate our own small businesses selling just one product: ourselves. We accept employment opportunities, negotiate rates when possible, and attempt to maximize profitability just like any small business. The big difference between freelance music and supplying paper products (ignoring the artistic differences) is that there is only one of us, and we can only be in one place at one time. Accepting employment with a particular organization for a given length of time also means turning down other concurrent employment offers for that same length of time. We musicians may have some impressive skills, but being in two places at the same time is not one of them.

With rare exception, the world of music is full of eager musicians willing to take one's place in the gig queue. Say "no" to a contractor and he or she will go with the next person in the queue. Say no enough times and one is permanently replaced by that person. Since taking one gig means saying "no" to another, climbing the gig ladder necessarily means that one will fade from prominence in the eyes of some contractors. Can one re-establish oneself with these former contacts at some future date? Possibly…if some of the 50 other players "waiting in the wings" haven't ingratiated themselves with these contractors. Another truism about the freelance music business is that the better the work, the less of an obligation the contractor has to re-hire the same musicians time after time. Better work is almost always less secure work. The following is an all-too-common scenario in the life of a freelance musician:

Road Warrior Without an Expense Account

You are called to play for a month with a top-tier orchestra like the Chicago Symphony. This is an offer that few classical freelance musicians in Chicago would turn down. Being a successful musician, you are already booked up with two weeks of regional orchestra work (one contracted position, one substitute position) and three church gigs.

Backing out of this contracted week of work may or may not be a big deal, depending on the organization. The other non-contracted week of work and the three church gigs pose a dilemma, however. With rare exceptions, backing out of these gigs often labels this musician in the minds of contractors as an unreliable resource. When a contractor is hiring for the next gig, the fact that this musician backed out at the last minute will usually cloud his or her opinion. Subbing out of the same gig a second time in the future will not only be likely to end that musician's association with that contractor but also land him or her on that contractor's "do not call" list. The church gigs will simply get another name from the many other potential hires in town and keep calling that person for the indefinite future (I know—that's how I got a lot of my regular non-contracted gigs).

Does that mean that you shouldn't take the month of Chicago Symphony work? Of course not. You would be crazy not to jump at these opportunities. There are ramifications to doing so, however, and they can come back to haunt you. Let's say you keep getting offered repeated substitute work with the Chicago Symphony. You therefore keep turning down other gigs in order to work for the best group in town. The next season comes along, however, and the symphony holds an audition for the spot you have been subbing for. All of a sudden you are no longer needed. One look at your calendar and you discover that there is nothing but white (days with no gigs) for months to come.

This happens to *many* musicians. The work most classical music freelancers want is the top-tier symphonic work such as with the Chicago Symphony, Boston Symphony, and Philadelphia Orchestra. When such calls come in, musicians often put enormous pressure on them-

The Vicious Cycle

selves to say "yes" to these calls. These organizations are under no obligation to call you again, however, and you may find yourself high and dry with to work at all after a long spell of regular playing with one of these organizations.

Here's the overriding issue—freelance work is a competitive business, and while much of your success comes from your musical ability, a nearly equal amount comes from how savvy you are at balancing commitments, massaging egos, and simply just being in the right place at the right time. No matter how good you are, a political mistake (waiting a day to call a contractor back) or a musical mistake (blotching a major entrance) can have negative repercussions for your career across the board.

Remember—people talk. They talk about your positive qualities, and they talk about your negative qualities. And if they aren't talking about you at all, well… you may be finding yourself with a withering freelance career.

Not everybody succeeds in freelancing, often through no fault of their own. People become "hot players" in the eyes of contractors, only to find themselves in the middle of the heap a couple of years later. Why? Maybe a new player moved to town who had subbed with a better orchestra than you had. Maybe the contractor finally starts calling that violinist that started carpooling with him to gigs instead of you. Maybe you started subbing in a major orchestra and the church contractors forget about you. Maybe another player starts subbing in a major orchestra and everyone starts calling that person, forgetting about you. Maybe your ambition to take major auditions causes you to turn down one gig too many, knocking you down the call list.

The best work for a freelancer is usually offered inconsistently and with little guarantee of future employment. Taking top-tier work gives a musician the most satisfaction and is impossible to resist. The dynamic nature of all freelance work often means that removing oneself from the eyes of any contractor can decrease the chances of being hired by that contractor again. Taking a better gig, therefore, often means losing a worse gig. If that better (but inconsistently offered) gig dries up, the musician can wind up without any gigs. The best players can usually re-establish those contacts, but the large number of available players makes this challenging.

Finally, many contractors are not interested in who is the best, only in who is *available* and *consistent*. Say "no" too many times and you are labeled unavailable. Sub out too many times and you are labeled inconsistent. It doesn't matter how good you are—you will remove yourself from many contractor's lists by moving up the gig chain. It is unavoidable, unfortunate, and a real hurdle for those pursuing a career in freelance performing.

Rats in the Ivory Tower

The Hidden Costs of Adjunct University Teaching

In my previous life as an adjunct university instructor, I was compensated at a rate of $35 per hour for each student I taught. This rate is comparable to many other public universities in the United States. Since this figure is a common hourly rate for many universities, it serves as a good illustrative example for the first of the many employment situation analyses that follow.

In addition to the $35 per hour lesson, I was paid a $635 retainer fee each semester for recruiting and other activities. This list of activities expected to be undertaken in order to receive said compensation included:

- Instrumental seminar classes (requiring an extra round trip to the university)
- Recruitment drives in local schools
- Attendance at student juries (another extra round trip)
- Audition days for prospective students
- Open houses

Road Warrior Without an Expense Account

For the purposes of this analysis, let's assume that two additional round trips per month were required of me in order to fulfill these expectations—in reality the number of days was probably higher than that in any given month.

The resulting compensation varied from term to term depending on my student load. My student load vacillated between four and ten students during my employment in this position. The resulting compensation (including retainer fee) ranged from $625 to $1050 per month.

Neither the hourly rate nor the retainer fee increased during my five years of employment (and has still not increased at this particular institution as of this writing), an unfortunately all-too-common occurrence in adjunct jobs such as this. While tenure track faculty members and lecturers at universities receive yearly cost-of-living salary increases, adjunct faculty members do not typically receive an increase in compensation on any regular basis, often working at the same institution for a decade or more at the exact same rate. This lack of cost of living increases means that adjunct faculty members actually get paid less each year regardless of their job performance. The only way to increase compensation under these circumstances is to hustle for more students, a practice that is, at best, dubious (for reasons that shall be explored in later chapters).

For the following exercise, we shall use the figure of $900 a month in total compensation for hourly lessons plus the aforementioned retainer fee as an illustrative example. This figure is on the upper end of what I was paid monthly for this university position. If I were to make one trip per week to teach, this would break down to $225 per day of teaching—not bad. This boils down to about 6.5 hours of teaching if I could line up the students back to back. In reality, however, it was impossible to get all of those students lined up one after another, so my time spent on the job was closer to 8.5 hours, lowering my average hourly compensation to $26.50.

Now comes the kicker—mileage. I lived 93 miles from this particular institution, making my round trip daily commute 186 miles. Much of this was on a two-lane highway, putting my commute time at a minimum of two hours on each leg of the trip (four hours total per day).

Adding those four additional commute hours put my weekly commitment at 12.5 hours, thus lowering my hourly compensation to $18 per hour. This is considerably lower than the original $35/hour figure (which is a fairly low compensation figure to begin with).

Figuring in my mileage….oh wait, I got no mileage! So, 44.5 cents per mile must therefore be taken off of that $900 monthly compensation figure. Years of brake jobs, oil changes, blown tires, cracked windshields and the like have taught me that the federal mileage rate really is what it costs you in the long run to drive to gigs.

Road Warrior Without an Expense Account

186 miles/trip x .445	$82.77 mileage/trip
$82.77 mileage/trip x 4 trips/month	$331.08 mileage/month
$900 - $331.08 mileage/month	**$568.92 monthly compensation after mileage**

Ouch! Mileage takes quite a bite out of your earnings, doesn't it? Driving is what really destroys the earnings of freelancers. I have driven 40,000-50,000 miles per year for the past seven years working sometimes in six states each year to earn a living. My pre-expenses income has been pretty handsome some years, but when actual costs are figured, the earnings always plummet to coffee shop employee levels (if not worse).

Let's break it down a little further.

If I were to travel only once a week (four trips per month):

$568.92 divided by 4	$142.23 per day
$142.23 divided by 12.5 hours	**$11.38 per hour**

Note that this does not include those extra trips to fulfill the requirements of the adjunct retainer fee. If I did only one extra trip per month:

$568.92 divided by 5	$113.78 per day
$113.78 divided by 12.5 hours	**$9.10 per hour**

If I made *two* extra trips per month (a far more realistic assessment of the requirements of teaching, seminars, juries, open houses, audition days, and other recruiting activities):

Rats in the Ivory Tower

$568.92 divided by 6	$94.82 per day
$94.82 divided by 12.5 hours	**$7.59 per hour**

These figures do not count any preparation hours and are also a low estimate of what it took to technically fulfill the adjunct retainer fee. Making $8-10 an hour (with no benefits, no raises....ever) is a lowly income for anybody in any field. Tens of thousands of dollars poorer (due to bachelors and masters degrees from Northwestern University—and that's with considerable student aid!) and 12 years later, I found myself toiling for the exact same wages I made as a file clerk in 1994.

Not only that, but I had to compete against other ambitious applicants for the *privilege* of making 1994 file clerk wages. The likelihood of even getting an opportunity to work for peanuts would likely not have presented itself without my fancy designer degrees.

Remember, this is pre-tax and is devoid of a pension contribution or any other benefit. Also, this figure assumes that I earned $900 monthly from this job. I frequently earned less than this figure per month during my time in this position, but my commuting costs remained the same (or increased with the steady rise in gasoline prices). This is another unfair drawback to pay-per-student teaching—when a student quits, your hourly wage drops a dollar or two, putting pressure on the pay-per-student adjunct teacher to lower his or her standards and pass unqualified students to keep the wage from dropping from coffee shop worker scale to dishwasher scale.

This low figure is more disturbing given the required advanced degrees an applicant is expected to have just to get an interview for an adjunct teaching position. When I applied for this position, I had two music performance degrees from Northwestern University and had taken nearly $40,000 in loans (not counting what my parents had to pay) which I was just staring to pay back.

The sad reality of the state of this profession is even more telling when looking at the highly qualified pool of applicants interested in filling my previous position. I was told by my colleagues at the university that this particular adjunct teaching position received the most number of applicants for any adjunct position in this institution's history. People with doctoral degrees and people with significant International Conference of Symphony and Opera Orchestras (ICSOM) orchestral experience were among the applicants.

One may criticize my decision for accepting employment at an institution that was so far from my home. Although my compensation would undoubtedly have increased if I had lived closer to this institution, it is simply impossible to find a happy medium between teaching venues and performance venues for many freelance musicians. The erratic nature of employment and lack of any long-term guarantee of employment (adjunct instructors are generally hired on yearly contracts and their position can be offered to another individual for any reason) also makes relocating for one of these positions unwise.

This job also happened to be the only significant double bass university teaching position to open up in the greater Chicago area during those years, and I consider myself lucky to have gotten the job. Also, my mileage was actually *less* than some other adjunct faculty members from this institution, and my student load (and thus my compensation) was higher than most adjunct faculty members, meaning that I actually drove less and earned more than many of my colleagues. Driving 50-80 miles one way for a job like this is very common here in the metropolitan Chicago area, and my cost/benefit breakdown thus serves as a representative model of the true cost of this kind of employment.

Private Teaching

Incorporating Private Instruction into the Freelance Career

Most professional musicians engage in at least some degree of private teaching. The tradition of passing down skills, knowledge, and experience from generation to generation in a one-on-one setting has been happening for hundreds of years. Musicians for the past several hundred years have derived a substantial amount of their income from private teaching, and this practice has continued to the present day, with musicians from organizations ranging from the New York Philharmonic to the Southeastern Palatine Symphony engaged in the art and craft of teaching.

Some musicians avoid teaching for a myriad of reasons. Inexperience, disinterest, and a lack of consistent availability are among the chief factors in a musician's choice to not teach privately. More often than not, however, performing musicians choose to teach at least a few students.
Financial considerations aside, private teaching can have a positive effect on both the attitude and psyche of the performing musician.

Working with young minds helps to put one's own technical and musical issues in perspective, and the act of communicating musical and technical concepts to develop and shape young performers can help inspire the teacher as well as the student. Forcing oneself to learn how to teach repertoire to students can help to give clarity to the teacher's own conceptions of the piece, making lessons a win-win situation for both parties involved.

I don't want to sugar-coat private teaching. There are lots of students out there who are not exactly founts of inspiration for teachers (and vice-versa), and lessons that don't have both parties engaged in the activity can be a real drag. Full-time orchestral performers can usually cherry-pick their students more than part-time or freelance performers, allowing for a handful of students that do provide the sort of satisfaction and musical stimulation that good performers and teachers crave.

The whole notion of differentiating between performer/teacher and performer is a somewhat modern notion. In my younger years, I remember poring over the Northwestern University doctoral dissertations during my free time and being amused at how many had titles like:

Domenico Scarlatti: Performer/Teacher – Teacher/Performer

Fernando Sor: Performer/Teacher – Teacher/Performer

Pablo Casals:Performer/Teacher – Teacher/Performer

Most musicians of previous generations were, to some degree, teachers, just like most musicians from these generations would be classified as freelancers today.
Delving into teaching in a book dedicated to the topic of being a freelance musician is a bit dicey, which is why it is essential to lay out the groundwork at the beginning for the examples that follow. Having a "teaching career" can mean so many things, and there are a myriad of divergent paths for teaching musicians. The following is a brief sum-

mary and analysis of some of the various roles that a teaching musician inhabits. These categories are fluid, and musicians may inhabit several of them during the course of their careers. Some may straddle the line between two categories or simultaneously work in several separate categories. Generally, however, musicians find themselves predominantly functioning in one or two of the categories described in the following pages.

1. Full-Time Orchestra Musicians Who Also Teach

These musicians have primary sources of income from performing jobs but still engage in some sort of private teaching. This can vary from just having a student or two on the weekends to holding down a university studio with a dozen performance majors. These teachers may be the best kinds of instructors for a student interested in obtaining an orchestra job. They are intimately connected with the art of performance and can relate the experiences they are having on the job at that exact moment to the student, allowing for a window into the life of professional performing musicians and lending a great deal of credibility to their advice.

The busy lifestyle associated with holding down a full-time performing job while teaching can make for periods of great stress and difficulty for these teachers. The teachers may be full of relevant and invaluable information but may often struggle to manage time and balance performing and teaching. Many individuals with good scheduling and time-management skills can handle this load without a problem, but it can be a real struggle for others.
While full-time orchestra musicians may sometimes concurrently fill tenure-track positions at universities, they much more frequently hold adjunct positions at these universities.

I put musicians with salaried, full-time orchestra jobs in their own category because these musicians rarely view their teaching as their primary source of income. It can be a supplement (sometimes a very nice supplement) to their primary income stream, and these musicians may in fact depend on this income to pay the bills (especially those musicians in orchestra jobs with more modest salaries), but the fact that they have a primary income stream makes them more independent than the freelance musician. Also, the fact that they hold a full-time orchestra position tends to automatically lend a degree of prestige and credibility that the freelance musician lacks.

2. Full-Time University Instrumental Instructors

These musicians hold positions dedicated (largely or fully) to private teaching. The responsibilities of the instructors vary greatly from university to university. Larger institutions will often employ instructors solely to teach a specific instrument and run a studio class, while smaller institutions will often have instrumental faculty double as theory, history, and ear training instructors. These instructors may be just as busy as the full-time orchestra musicians who also teach, but their activities are usually more focused around their particular academic institutions, and, as such, they are likely more frequently available and accessible to the student.

For some instruments (and double bass is certainly one of them), the beliefs and approaches of many non-orchestral university faculty members do not gel with the beliefs and approaches of the majority of orchestral musicians, and students must take care when selecting a teacher if they are interested in securing a position in a full-time orchestra.
Is it bad if these beliefs don't gel? It all boils down to a matter of perspective. If one assumes that the core skill set necessary for musical success is not tied to the orchestral experience, then studying with a teacher without extensive experience in this musical medium may not be a priority. If one assumes that preparation for a career in orchestral performance is contingent on a close instructional relationship with an experienced orchestral professional, however, the experience of the teacher in the professional orchestral world becomes paramount.

3. Part-Time University Instrumental Instructor

People in these jobs make up the dark underbelly of higher education, working deep below the ivory tower of academia in the salt mines, usually earning modest wages and rarely receiving benefits. This particular component of the freelancer employment suite was covered extensively in Chapter 6 of this book.

4. K-12 Music Instructor

This particular form of teacher employment is really a career path of its own, and it does not really fall within the scope of private instruction. Becoming a K-12 teacher requires qualifications distinct from the other types of employment described in this book, and it is therefore unlikely that many musicians on a path toward a full-time orchestral position will possess the qualifications for attaining such employment. Taking a wider view, however, it quickly becomes apparent that many musicians who participate in the world of orchestral freelancing hold K-12 teaching positions as well. Combining some freelancing with a part-time or full-time job as an elementary or secondary school music teacher can make for a stable and satisfying lifestyle, and such musicians are able to find a great balance between performing and teaching. This career path is a third option for musicians seeking to balance the security (pension, benefits, vacation, sick leave) of a full-time job with their work in the world of the performing arts.

Unfortunately, there is a perception among other music performers that musicians who teach in K-12 elementary or secondary education positions are not good performers. This is an unfortunate perception, but it is a common one nevertheless. Musical talent is independent of current employment (some of the best double bassists I know are full-time web developers, for example), and most musicians realize this fact. Anyone who thinks that the life of a full-time freelancer (50,000 miles in 2006 for me, with similar mileage racked up in previous years) provides for more practice time than the life of a schoolteacher engaging in self delusion, and combining such a job with regular performing can make for a great musical life.

5. Private Music School/Music Store Instructor

These teachers are hired through an existing organization to provide instruction to students at their facility. Students usually pay the organization directly, which then pays the teachers after taking a percentage of their earnings (typically 30-50%) for administrative purposes.

The upside to this arrangement is that teachers usually have to just show up and teach. Managing a large studio is like running a small business, and having someone to take care of these details can often be worth the massive cut these organizations take from one's earnings.

It can be difficult to make a living working only in one of these teaching jobs (unlike the other jobs on the list) due to the fact that you are often working at half the rate of other non-institute colleagues. These private music school/music store instructors have a role very similar to that of a freelance musician.

6. Private Studio Instructor

There is a quiet army of private studio instructors out there in the world, peering out from behind their curtains, cats sitting on the piano, stacks of Suzuki books on every available surface. They teach kids before school, after school, and on the weekends. They may perform in a select few groups, but the vast majority of their income comes from private instruction.

Running your own private studio involves inhabiting the roles of both teacher and business manager (as alluded to before), and it is actually a very different trajectory than any of the others described. These people have essentially started their own small businesses, and their independence from performance income puts them in a very different camp from the freelancers/teachers described below. These teachers usually have much more consistent schedules but without the thrills (and duds) of life as performers.

7. *Traveling/House Call Teachers*

I remember seeing fleets of Ford Escort wagons double parked, flashers on, all over my former neighborhood in Chicago in the 1990s. One fleet of Escorts was operated by a company called Dial-a-Maid, and the other was operated by a company called Music Teachers at Home. Both fleets seemed to be driven by harried-looking individuals (actually, the Dial-a-Maid folks looked more relaxed and happier).

Being a "hobo teacher" has some pluses and some minuses. I do my fair share of this kind of teaching, and I actually don't mind it. I think of it as a series of 'mini-gigs' all in a row, and the little break traveling between people's places helps to reset my mind and leave me fresh for the next lesson.
The downside? Well, it doesn't take much for you to start feeling like the maid. You are, after all, hired help to some degree (albeit more like a tutor than a maid), but there is a big difference psychologically (to the teacher, at least) between being in charge of your classroom/studio and being that guy that comes between the paper boy and the lawn maintenance guy.

How These Roles are Inhabited by the Freelance Performers/Teachers

Freelance performers teach under many different circumstances and with many different roles. To me, freelance performers/teachers use the type of part-time performing work described earlier in this book (regional orchestras, work from contractors, substitute/extra work in major symphonies) as the core of their income, and supplement it with teaching. This reliance on income from freelance/ad hoc performance creates a lifestyle and a set of circumstances quite different from the other teaching roles described above. Adjunct teaching positions typically fall to either full-time orchestra musicians or else to freelance performers/teachers, and, as such, they make up a piece of the freelance puzzle for many musicians.

Freelance performers/teachers may do some of the work described above such as private music school/music store instructors, traveling/house call teachers, adjunct university teaching, teach private lessons in a public school (either during or after school hours), teach out of one's home, or do a combination of all of these types of teaching. Performers/teachers often arrange their private lesson schedule around gigs and other obligations, creating an ad hoc schedule much like their performing schedule.

Benefits of Private Teaching for the Freelance Musician

Amalgamating teaching into a freelance career makes sense on many fronts. Simply put, gigs are sporadic and can fall through, pay late, or dry up with little warning. Also, the mileage most freelance musicians put on their vehicles while doing such work is considerable, and this cuts massively into the profit of musicians. Teaching tends to involve much less driving and is much more stable, and it therefore provides an excellent employment cushion for the freelance musician. Benefits include:

Stable, Reliable Income - For many people, teaching can provide a steady stream of income to freelancers and a financial foundation upon which to build their performing work. This has certainly been the case for me over the past decade. As I look back on tax returns for the last several years, I notice that no matter how many gigs I take, my income from performing has remained stagnant or risen only modestly. My teaching income, however, has risen dramatically over the last five years, largely because of my diversification into adjunct university teaching, house-call teaching, and teaching private lessons in the public schools.

Schedule Control - With so many elements of the freelance musician's schedule in a state of constant flux, it is nice to have at least one thing under your control. Although many factors dictate when lessons occur (school schedules, availability of facilities), the freelance teacher has at least some degree of control to say when these lessons will take place, often filling a hole that would not normally be taken up with a gig. Making what would otherwise be downtime profitable is one of the keys to financial success in the freelance world, and teaching is, for most musicians, one of the main methods of boosting income.

Less Driving - Non-freelancers may not understand why references to driving occur so frequently throughout this book. Well, for most freelance musicians, the time spent on the road far exceeds the time spent actually working. Many Chicago-area freelance musicians work in many neighboring states, a common fact of life for freelance musicians in most regions of the United States. It is not uncommon for a freelance musician to work one week in Illinois, the next week in Wisconsin, the following week in Michigan, and the week after that in Indiana. Over the years, I have often found myself working in southern Tennessee one night and then having to jump in the car and drive all night to make it to Wisconsin for a rehearsal the next day. For many freelancers, this kind of wacko thing is a normal part of being a musician. Me? I hate it, and I am convinced that it takes a month off of my life expectancy every time I do it.

Problems with Combining Teaching and Freelance Performing

For the freelance musician, the benefits of teaching far outweigh the drawbacks. Under good circumstances, private teaching can be a very efficient way to double the weekly take-home pay of the freelance musician. Intelligent scheduling of students combined with an active gigging lifestyle can make for a stable and satisfying career for many freelance musicians. There are, though, a few problems worth briefly touching upon:

Bad scheduling - You need to guard against over scheduling or inefficient scheduling when combining freelance performing and teaching. It is very easy to fall into the trap of scheduling people with wide spaces between lessons, making a trip to a distant music school to teach only one or two students, or to otherwise invite complications into the scheduling process. You must be careful to weigh the benefits and drawbacks of accepting students who do not neatly fit into the performer/teacher's schedule, particularly once the teacher's studio begins to grow. If you must devote three hours for travel time plus lesson time, the hourly rate has actually been reduced to 1/3 of what it would be were the students scheduled back-to-back in a home studio.

Creating a private teaching schedule is one giant balancing act requiring cajoling, pleading, and compromising, and adding a variable gig schedule into the mix is like throwing a cat into a hamster cage—total chaos.

Inconsistent Lesson Schedule - I am constantly canceling lessons for gigs. The more students I have, the bigger a problem this becomes. When musicians consider themselves performers first and foremost, their performance activity usually receives higher priority than scheduled teaching obligations. Rescheduling thus becomes a major concern for the freelance performer/teacher.

Constant rescheduling is detrimental to both student and teacher. Having consistent, regular lessons each week is an established method for advancing the craft of instrumental musicianship, and having to skip weeks or cram several lessons only few days apart to make up missed lessons reduces the effectiveness of these lessons.

Here's the bottom line—if you are an active performer, you *will* be canceling lessons. If you teach at a university or music school which requires "x" number of lessons per semester, you may be in for some make-up pain. At my former university job 93 miles away from my home, I would sometimes start teaching make-ups at 7 p.m. (after a full day of performing and teaching other students) and teach until midnight, then drive two hours home and be up by 6 a.m. to drive out to the Chicago suburbs and start teaching again.

Zombification - Performing takes time. Teaching takes time. The gigs come in, but inconsistently. The teaching calls come in with their performer/teachers who teach 50, 60, 70 or more private lessons each week in addition to their gig schedule. Approaching those sorts of numbers for weekly lessons removes virtually all time for personal practice and development, chamber music, and other essential aspects of the creative and professional life of an artist.

Some of these teachers manage to handle all these myriad responsibilities plus keep their practicing up; but more often than not these people become "teaching zombies," wandering the halls of the local high school, eyes red, mouth hanging open, searching for a cup of coffee between lessons, not keeping up their craft, and stagnating or declining musically.

I realize that musicians need to earn a living, and I wouldn't begrudge anyone's desire to maximize earning potential by taking on huge numbers of students. I used to teach 40 students per week and should therefore at least receive an honorable mention in the teaching zombie club! I also believe, however, that if performer/teachers do not keep up their craft, always striving to improve their own playing and further hone their abilities, they have less to offer the student and are acting as a questionable role model for the future performing artist.

Burnout

But the biggest problem of all, and one that is different from the zombification described above, is burnout—the subject of the following chapter; this problem neutralizes more freelancers than any other.

8

Burnout

Burning the Freelance Candle at Both Ends

A good friend of mine told me as I started my freelance career that musicians can only last ten years as freelancers. After approximately ten years, most freelancers hang up their hat and look for other means of employment.

"Bah!" I said.

I was a tough cookie, able to put in six, seven, or eight hours in the practice room plus play gigs and do other activities. As long as the freelance doors kept opening, I could keep doing this indefinitely. Surely I'd end up with a job before ten years were up, and, if not, I could keep up this lifestyle as long as I wanted to.

But here I find myself, just about ten years after having that conversation with my friend, trying like crazy to get out of this freelancing lifestyle.

What a wimp I am, right?

Burnout

Playing music is not an easy way to make a living. I think that this is a fairly obvious fact. If a person wants to make some bucks and have a stable life, then that person is in the wrong profession. This is a given that was presented in earlier chapters, and it is an assumption that I hope people keep in the back of their mind during the remainder of this book.

Given the fact that we musicians are not in it for the money and remain professional musicians despite the financial and lifestyle struggles, what are the trends in this business of which we need to be aware?

Well, the main trend that I am attempting to document in this series is that traditional performance employment opportunities in the world of classical music—primarily orchestral and academic positions, but other positions as well—are shrinking. Full-time orchestras continue to cut back, go bankrupt, and disappear, and they are (with the occasional extremely rare exception) never replaced.

- ❖ Jobs are disappearing.
- ❖ Competition is increasing.
- ❖ Things are getting worse, not better.

Welcome to the club. Here's a coupon for 10% off your next oil change. You're going to need it.

The topic of gig circles that exist within most major metropolitan areas was analyzed in depth in Chapter Two. Many times, the gig circle one inhabits determines longevity for the freelance musician before burning out. Musicians who regularly substitute in top-tier orchestras, play touring shows, perform in the top area regional orchestras, and are the top call for the area contractors can very easily have the financial stability and artistic satisfaction of a member of a major full-time orchestra (albeit without the stability or benefits that this sort of position confers). They may teach a few students on the side who pay a premium for the expertise of such a player. Such individuals are likely to keep their creative and professional energies active much longer

For each major metropolitan area, only a select few players on each instrument can inhabit this top gig circle. Everyone else must inhabit different gig circles from this rarified clique and must deal with the extra driving, lower pay, and less artistically satisfying conditions that these other circles inevitably offer.

Even freelancers in the top gig circles are not immune to the frustrations, conflicts, and perils of all the aspects of freelancing, including problems with balancing regional orchestras, duking it out with full-time orchestra musicians for extra work, massaging the egos of contractors, or squeezing private teaching into all the available schedule cracks. These are problems that all freelancers face, and as jobs grow ever scarcer and high-quality performers graduate from music school in ever greater numbers, with nary a job in sight, competition for even these top-tier freelance spots will increase, altering the landscape for current freelancers and making the search for steady work a constant competitive struggle.

It's All About the Car

This, ultimately, is what destroys freelancers. That damnable time spent in the vehicle, driving home across state lines, with only truck drivers, deer, and inebriated drivers to keep the musician company. More often than not, the time spent in the car exceeds the time spent on stage rehearsing or performing. It's like an office worker commuting four hours each way to work for 2 ½ hours.

Burnout

Freelancers pass those driving hours in various ways. Many long-haul musicians are hardcore audio books fans (I went through a pretty serious audio books phase myself during my time on the road), gobbling up a couple of unabridged novels each week playing gigs. Others talk on the phone to pass the time. I get many calls around midnight (or later) from colleagues on their way home from who knows what far-flung city, looking for a little company to help pass the hours.

Many people call this type of work "driving for dollars," which is an apt description of this lifestyle. While freelancing, I will often see the same haggard faces in central Wisconsin as I did the week before in northern Indiana, and I know that I will be seeing them again the following week in central Illinois and two months later in southern Iowa. I will often find myself on gigs 90 miles from my home in Evanston, with over half of the musicians of the group also residing in Evanston. I joke to these musicians that we should have all saved ourselves the trip and rehearsed in my living room!

and they shorten the career of a freelance musician faster than any other element.

I personally have countless horror stories of commuting all over the country, covering four states in one month, bouncing around the entire country, from South Carolina all the way to Oregon in the space of a couple of months. My final year of freelancing, I was on my fourth car in seven years, having put close to 400,000 miles on these vehicles during that time span.

Actually, "driving for dollars" is too kind a term for this kind of work. Guess how much I have been compensated for that half-million miles? Not much, that's for sure. I have never once in my freelance career been paid the federal standard for mileage, with most of my work paying either no mileage or else less than half of the federal rate. If you want to see some more detailed figures on the impact that this kind of driving has on your bottom line, go back and read Chapter 6. Then go bang your head against a concrete piling to ease your depression from seeing these statistics.

I decided to call it quits on this full-time freelance lifestyle during the summer of 2006. A combination of factors player into this decision—getting married, turning 30, and the slow, creeping realization that I had fallen into a freelance quagmire. I could pay my bills and keep food on the table, but visualizing another decade of driving 50,000 miles each year, all-night frantic dashes across the country in the dead of winter, and an endless stream of interchangeable pick-up gigs and low-quality community orchestra engagements made me shudder. I am still basically doing this work full-time at present, but I am exploring some other career options at the same time. I have always known that this kind of lifestyle (freelance musician/driver) was not for me, and each passing year only makes this fact clearer.

What may be of considerable interest to readers is what happened to my bottom line when I dropped a lot of my work—it went up! After

Burnout

quitting my university jobs and my long-haul drives, I actually had *more* money in my pocket than I did when I was working all of these jobs.

Do you know what that means?

It means that much of this physically exhausting, nerve-wracking, highly unsatisfying lifestyle was actually costing me money.

I'll delve deeper into the ramifications of this realization and what I think that freelancers can do to be smarter about their professional commitments in the final chapter of this book, but I can say that, for me, I was unwittingly performing a form of musical charity with much of my work, giving my money away to the Illinois and Indiana toll systems, the oil industry, and countless other institutions. I was actually *paying* for the dubious pleasure of traversing the American Midwest on my own dime.

If much of my work ended up being this kind of "charity work," how many other freelancers are in the same boat? A lot, I'll bet.

This lifestyle is hard. It makes it very difficult to have a family or any semblance of a "normal" life. We musicians choose this lifestyle, of course, and we are therefore ultimately responsible for accepting the resulting conditions. Too many of us, however, get so caught up chasing our "dream job" in a symphony orchestra that we forsake family, friends, and eventually the seeds of those things which can contribute to a much more satisfying life, all for the chance to play in an orchestra.

Burnout

Is it worth it?

Think about it—is it *really* worth it?

For many people, it is. They are willing to pay the dues, put in t
time, make the sacrifices, do the rounds, and take each and ever
portunity to move forward toward their dream. For many peopl
works out, and they end up in a fulfilling and meaningful emplo
situation. For others, they may obtain a position in an orchestra
to later realize that their organization is deficient in some way—
musically, monetarily, or structurally—and they feel trapped, un
obtain another job due to the rigors of the audition circuit and ur
ing to abandon their current job and a life as an orchestral musician.
They are miserable and stuck.

Others never land that coveted full-time orchestral position. They continue either to chase after it well into their 40s and 50s, settle into a life of freelancing, or get out of music altogether.

Still others never wanted to land an orchestra gig in the first place. Never having had that expectation of a full-time orchestra job waiting for them, they decide to create their own opportunities for themselves.

Rethinking Music Performance Degrees

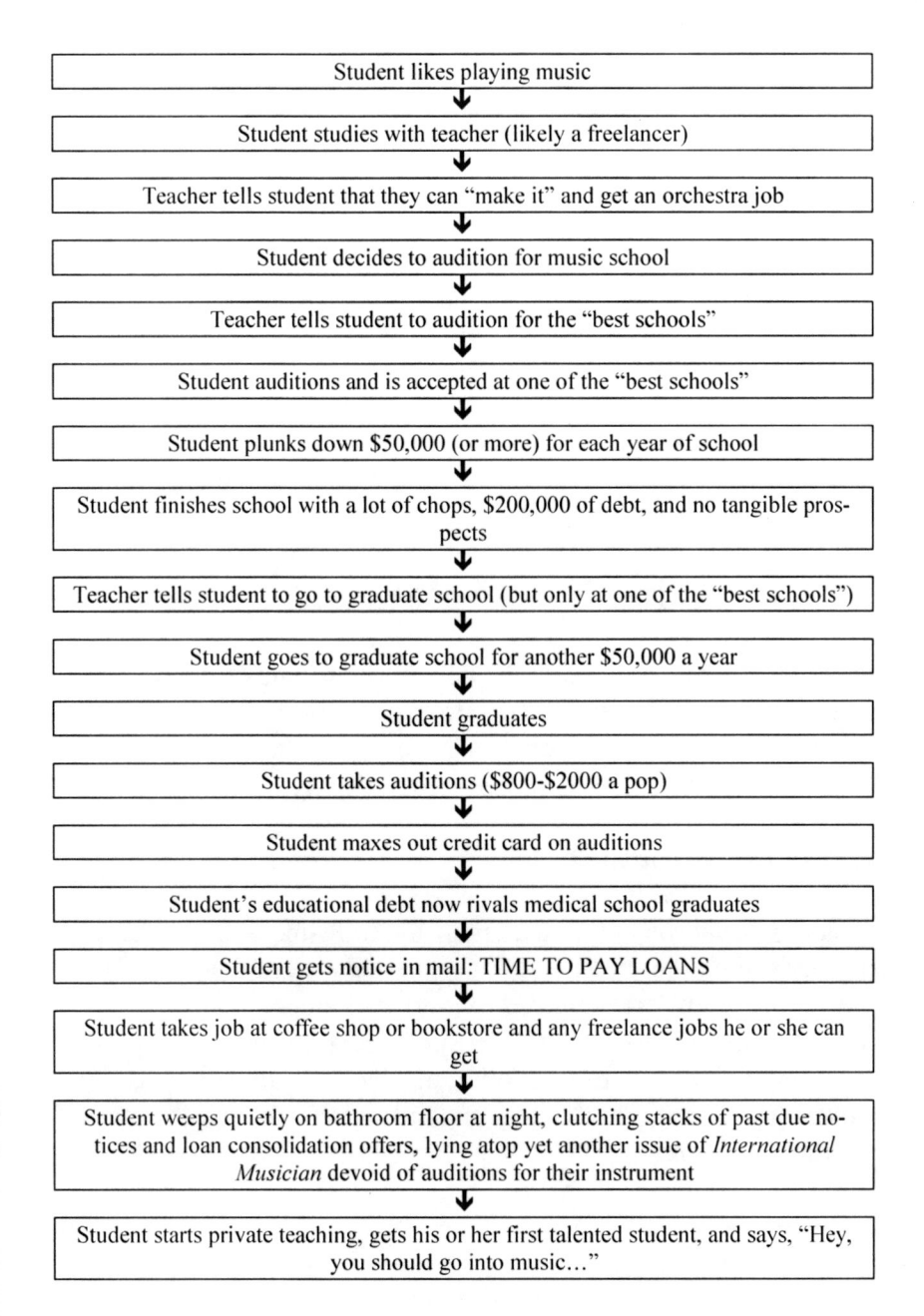

Student likes playing music
↓
| Student studies with teacher (likely a freelancer) |
↓
| Teacher tells student that they can "make it" and get an orchestra job |
↓
| Student decides to audition for music school |
↓
| Teacher tells student to audition for the "best schools" |
↓
| Student auditions and is accepted at one of the "best schools" |
↓
| Student plunks down $50,000 (or more) for each year of school |
↓
| Student finishes school with a lot of chops, $200,000 of debt, and no tangible prospects |
↓
| Teacher tells student to go to graduate school (but only at one of the "best schools") |
↓
| Student goes to graduate school for another $50,000 a year |
↓
| Student graduates |
↓
| Student takes auditions ($800-$2000 a pop) |
↓
| Student maxes out credit card on auditions |
↓
| Student's educational debt now rivals medical school graduates |
↓
| Student gets notice in mail: TIME TO PAY LOANS |
↓
| Student takes job at coffee shop or bookstore and any freelance jobs he or she can get |
↓
| Student weeps quietly on bathroom floor at night, clutching stacks of past due notices and loan consolidation offers, lying atop yet another issue of *International Musician* devoid of auditions for their instrument |
↓
| Student starts private teaching, gets his or her first talented student, and says, "Hey, you should go into music…" |

And the cycle repeats itself.

Loan balances rivaling those of medical students.

Multiple degrees with vague practical application.

Overeducated and underemployed.

Bitter and angry.

Broke and desperate.

Is this the way it has to be? No! There is another path, another orientation, a healthier way to approach the pursuit of a professional life in music performance.

What is the Solution?

It's simple. In order to succeed in the contemporary musical landscape, classical music performers need to become businessmen or businesswomen as much as performers, promoters as much as practice room hermits, and innovators as much as reproducers.

They need to become entrepreneurs.

If one looks back in time before the era of the full-time orchestra as a primary means of employment (pre-1960), it is apparent that the concept of musician as entrepreneur has existed ever since music itself. Musicians of yesteryear existed professionally as freelancers, weaving a combination of playing jobs with other musical activities such as teaching, accompanying, conducting, and arranging to create the tapestry of their musical lives.

Classical musicians need to think of themselves as independent contractors, as small businesses servicing a wide variety of musical needs. This is the most likely scenario for professional musicians looking into the future.

Rethinking Music Performance Degrees

Opportunity abounds for the intrepid musician. When I look around this vibrant city of Chicago, I see possibilities everywhere. Without a doubt, musicians *can* succeed and prosper in the music world. We just need to refocus and change our outlook.

In order to refocus, musicians need to attack the problem at its core. The biggest problem facing classical musicians today is that, with rare exceptions, our music conservatory system does a reprehensible job preparing music students for today's professional landscape. The core music curriculum at schools today, while providing a path to individual instrumental prowess and a general and theoretical understanding of the underpinning of our art form, gives us virtually no training in specifically *how* to make a career in this business.

The inadequate professional training provided by music schools is understandable when reflecting upon the background of most university instrumental faculty. If they are full-time members of professional symphony orchestras, they are one of the lucky 1/10 of one percent who made it through the audition process into a full-time orchestra gig. What is the advice that these people dole out?

"If I made it, so can you!"

This is advice that is at best extremely irresponsible and, at worst, malicious and disastrous to the naïve student. As a musician, you are trained your whole life to do one thing—listen to your teacher! When your teacher says "go for it!," you go for it. You do it even if that "going for it" has a price tag of $50,000 or more each year.

Fast-forward four years and $200,000 later. You get a pat on the back, a handshake, and a degree.
What do you do now? Hit the audition scene, right? It will cost the bass player somewhere between $800 and $2000 to take a typical orchestra audition.

Road Warrior Without an Expense Account

You open the American Federation of Musicians monthly paper and page through the job ads. Where are the jobs? You page through again, your heart racing. There aren't any auditions!

With no job, no prospects, no money, and two hundred thousand dollars in debt, you are trained to do only one thing: take and win auditions that are statistically nearly impossible to obtain.

Thanks, music school!

Few can dispute the effectiveness of the modern conservatory/music department system in producing high quality performers. Standards have risen in the last 50 years on virtually every instrument; what was considered to be extraordinary technical acumen in the early 20th century is now par for the course at most music schools. More music students competing for fewer positions have undoubtedly helped to raise technical standards worldwide.

A case can certainly be made for music schools emphasizing technical mastery over true musical expression. Assessing progress in technical mastery is more cut-and-dried than measuring depth of musical development, and music schools join many other disciplines in rewarding cognitive and mechanical progress while ignoring affective maturation and development, but that is a discussion for another time.

Music schools, then, are doing a good job (despite the above concern in program emphasis) of producing graduates who are great performers, but a rotten job producing graduates with applicable job skills in today's musical environment.
It's like producing soldiers with no army for them to serve in, teachers with no schools for them to teach in, or business school graduates with no companies for them to work in. Training musicians to become great performers of symphonic literature but not providing them with any extra-musical skills for success in today's challenging employment market is irresponsible, shortsighted, and just plain lazy on the part of our academic institutions.

It is certainly *easier* to train musicians in traditional music school disciplines (theory, aural skills, applied lessons, ensembles, chamber music), add a smattering of pedagogy classes and some liberal arts trim, and send them out into the world with a pat on the back and a massive loan bill in the mail. The predominant curriculum for music performance majors fosters general musicianship, instrumental excellence, ensemble skills, and a degree of pedagogical knowledge but rarely requires coursework to teach the successful application of these skills.

Is There Another Way?

Yes—and a few music schools (most notably the Eastman School with their Orchestral Studies Diploma) are beginning to change course and offer an education more suited to today's challenging musical environment. What is needed is a redefinition of the music performance degree, a complete reorientation at the institutional level of what it means to be a performer and what sort of preparation and skill set development is necessary for a successful career as a performing entrepreneur. Some schools, like Eastman, are enacting progressive curriculum change in response to this evolving musical landscape. Most schools are not. This is a disservice to the students, the faculty, the industry, and the art itself. Training vast numbers of musicians for a career with a 5% success rate is a huge disservice to the other 95% of the student body. Would we tolerate a system where only 5% of graduating lawyers find employment in their field? How about 5% of graduating teachers, or business school graduates? Why should music be any different?

Notice the phrase from the previous paragraph: *performing entrepreneur*. This is the crux of it; if music students can be trained to generate their own opportunities and use their talent, enthusiasm, and young energy and spirit to create something new and propel the art forward, we may in fact have a sunny musical future. Opportunities abound in this field for those with the right skills and business acumen to generate their own opportunities and success. Academic institutions have a responsibility to their music performance students to ensure that learning these skills is a required part of their curricula.

While attending countless professional auditions during my career, I would frequently despair at all of the youthful energy and effort that is channeled into the orchestral audition scene. I wondered what the result would be if these musicians could take that energy and use it to create their own opportunities rather than try to fit into the employment structure created by our forefathers. Think of the possibilities!

This is the problem! We aren't taught in music school to be entrepreneurs—we're taught to be lemmings.

Even soloists are taught in this way. We are taught to become highly polished little cogs to fit into these giant decaying machines, musical industrial plants belching out the same tired old claptrap.

Exploring Other Alternatives

Before outlining alternatives, it is important to stress that creating a music school curriculum that has relevance and applicability to the contemporary employment landscape should not happen at the expense of musical and technical standards. Think of it as instrument smarts and street smarts. Music schools predominantly teach the former, and they need to teach both, but in doing so they should not make a slide towards street smarts at the expense of instrumental proficiency standards. Without an excellent musical product to offer, we all become snake oil salesmen, foisting a shabby product on the public and devaluing our craft in the process. We must not allow music conservatories to produce graduates with great business and marketing acumen but questionable musical skills. If the musical skills aren't there, the performance degree should not be awarded.

Also, these curriculum changes should be imposed only on the undergraduate music performance degree and should not affect masters or doctoral degrees in music performance. Studying music performance in and of itself has a great deal of value and merit, and these degrees are very useful for acquiring additional training and study on one's primary instrument as well as training a musician for a symphonic job or music performance university faculty position. But, much as medical students need to go through an undergraduate degree before attending medical school, music performance majors should receive a firm grounding in the practical skill set required to survive and adapt as a musician. Any graduate study of music performance would thereby be conducted with a firm grounding in the practical application of performance skills.

I do not believe that these curriculum changes should be imposed on music education students or musicology/theory/history students. This may be a point of contention, but the course of study in music education already provides a clear path to employment, and musicologists, music theorists, and music historians are on a path to academia that does not require as great a practical skill set as performers require.

Degrees awarded by institutions of higher education (colleges, universities, conservatories, trade schools) fall into two basic categories: theoretical and practical. Theoretical degrees include mathematics, history, linguistics, philosophy, and other such disciplines without a defined non-academic career path at the conclusion of the degree. Traditional liberal arts degrees are theoretical degrees intended to give the student knowledge of a broad spectrum of topics and comprehensive knowledge of one particular theoretical discipline. Although there may be several fields in which a recipient of a theoretical degree can successfully seek employment, there is not a specific career path tied to these jobs in the non-academic world.

Practical degrees include business, education, computer science, engineering, nursing, air conditioner repair, and other such disciplines with a set of specific jobs tied to that program of study. Go to nursing school, become a nurse; go to engineering school, become an engineer; go to air conditioner repair school, become an air conditioner repairman. While coursework for a practical degree may be quite theoretical in nature, the acquisition of that degree makes the graduate an attractive candidate for employment in one or more job fields.

There is always an academic career path to any field of study—one can study history, mathematics, or philosophy with the intent of teaching one of these subjects at a university. The very fact that it is possible to study a particular subject at the university level means that there is a path to employment for teaching that subject. The circular path of academic careers exists for every field, so it shall be ignored for the purposes of this article—every subject that exists by nature of its existence provides a career path toward the teaching of that subject.

Many music degrees clearly fit into either the practical or theoretical categories. Music education degrees, music technology, and music business degrees are practical degrees, while music theory, music history, and musicology degrees are theoretical degrees.

Music performance degrees are purported to be practical degrees, training the recipient to be a successful "doer" in the arts. These degrees are billed as practical degrees to incoming students, but the skill set taught within the traditional music performance degree curriculum is entirely theoretical in nature. There is therefore a huge disconnect between what is taught in the classroom and what happens in the real world. Music performance students think that they are getting a practical degree—go to school, get a job, play music—when in reality they are getting a theoretical degree.

Selling a theoretical degree as a practical degree does a huge disservice to students, and this practice creates a vicious cycle of qualified performers without opportunities and without the skill set to easily create their own opportunities. These opportunities include the following: creating their own performance organizations and setting up as a not-for-profit; writing grants; taking care of marketing and publicity; working with government agencies and arts advocacy agencies at the local, county, state, and federal level; booking and managing tours;

contracting; internet-based aspects of the music business; working with outlets to sell your own recordings; and setting up supplementary businesses relating to your art.

Opportunity abounds if the correct set of skills are taught to harness this opportunity. Why aren't music performance majors being taught these skills?

This situation needs to be changed—now.

In its current form, the music performance undergraduate degree is of dubious value, and it must be replaced by a more relevant and applicable degree. Undergraduate music performance degrees must incorporate elements of the current music performance curriculum with training in business, accounting, marketing, negotiating, public relations, and communications to create a new degree:

<u>Practical</u> Music Performance

10

Refocusing: Musical Entrepreneurship

Reinvigorating the Art Music Scene through Practical Music Performance

Where do we go from here? Do we all just turn in our instruments and quit this miserable business? Not me, and not you either, I imagine. We musicians know the value of what we do. We know that our art can change lives, create happiness, inspire greatness in others, and simply make the world a more beautiful place. We would sooner die than give up on this amazing language and means of communication.

But what is happening to this profession? How long can musicians reasonably expect to cobble together a living by playing with six part-time orchestras in four different states, driving 50,000 miles a year, living out of the car, sleeping in rest stops, with no benefits or future prospects and hundreds of thousands of dollars in student loans hanging over their heads?

Refocusing: Musical Entrepreneurship

Consider the following immutable aspects of the business:

- ❖ Employment in the classical music field necessitates musical study at the collegiate level.
- ❖ The cost of higher education has skyrocketed, outpacing even the rise in health care costs.
- ❖ Music performance degrees train musicians to do one thing very well.
- ❖ The demand for that "one thing" decreases with each year even as competition increases.
- ❖ Employment prospects hover in the single percentile
- ❖ Student loans rival those of medical school students

Something has to change.

For starters, we need to change the focus of the music performance degree to make it more applicable for contemporary music performance graduates. People no longer train to be telegraph operators or Victrola manufacturers. These businesses evolved. So must musicians.

The progressive disappearance of full-time orchestral jobs from the employment landscape is unfortunate; orchestral playing is a very satisfying profession, and many would love to do it full-time, provided that they received enough compensation to live a reasonable adult life. But those who drive 180 miles for a $70 gig (and more and more music graduates do exactly this every year) are not exactly setting themselves up for a prosperous future.

There's nothing wrong with paying dues. After all, many professions involve practitioners paying dues before reaping the eventual rewards of their career path. But classical music careers all too frequently dead end in that original $70 job. All too often, paying dues only results in paying more dues for less money the following year, and even more dues for even less the following year....

Only around 5% of music conservatory graduates connect with full-time employment in instrumental performance (and that success rate shrinks with each passing year). What happens to the other 95%?

Many leave the field of music, using their degree as they would any other liberal arts degree, entering the 9-to-5 world and pursuing a more traditional career path.
The rest are dumped (like rats in a bucket) into the freelance world, left to fend for themselves with nary a piece of cheese in plain view.

Connecting the Musical Dots

I chose this life. I chose to make a career out of music.

I just wish I had known.

I wish I had known how competitive the traditional path to satisfactory employment (a full-time orchestra position) is for the classical musician. Music schools rarely outline realistic employment statistics, prospects, and options for their students, clinging to traditional conservatory education principles from the late nineteenth century. Every other career field changes with and adapts to new circumstances—why not music?

Not adequately preparing music performance students as artists with business acumen is perhaps the greatest crime committed by the music conservatory system.

I wish that I had known what I could do besides get a job in a full-time orchestra when I was in music school. There was no formal component in any stage of my musical education (and I went to a well-renowned music school for both of my performance degrees) addressing real options for performing musicians.

Refocusing: Musical Entrepreneurship

After years in the freelance business, of course, I can rattle some of them off without batting an eye:

- Full-time orchestral employment (audition circuit)
- Part-time regional orchestra employment (audition circuit)
- Pick-up group orchestral employment (word-of-mouth)
- Church-related employment (contracting or being subcontracted)
- Corporate functions (contracting or being subcontracted)
- Recording work (sessions)
- Educational performance work (in-school performances, children's concerts)
- University teaching (full-time or adjunct)
- Private teaching (home, music school, within a school system)
- Contracting (orchestras, chamber groups, quartets, quintets, duos, trios)
- Contemporary music ensemble employment
- Summer institute teaching (perform and/or teach at music festival)
- Ballet orchestra employment
- Opera orchestra employment
- Side businesses (reed making, contracting, publishing arrangements, etc.)

These divergent options for generating income as a performer are addressed superficially, if at all, in most academic institutions. I did hear these phrases from time to time during my time as a music student:

"There are recording sessions!"

"There are auditions!"

"You know, sometimes musicians also teach."

"You should make contacts!"

What is rarely addressed is *how* any of these objectives are accomplished. It's not rocket science, and there *are* clear steps that can be taken to secure employment in any of the aforementioned career sub-paths.

Contracting

Any musical studies program with an emphasis in practical music performance absolutely requires the inclusion of a course on contracting. Interacting with existing contractors and starting your own contracting business is integral to the prosperity of many freelance musicians, and getting some practical advice in this public relations and networking endeavor would greatly benefit today's future professional musician.

Such a course should include the following topics:

1. What is contracting?
2. Who are the major contractors in the metropolitan area? (bringing in such figures to guest teach a class at this point would be a very good idea)
3. How does one go about setting up a contracting business?
    a. Legal ramifications of contracting/subcontracting
    b. Tax forms and other accounting necessities
    c. AFM union information
        i. Scale
        ii. Hours
        iii. Working conditions
        iv. Doubling
    d. Website development
    e. Obtaining engagements
4. Ethics and guidelines for contracting
    a. Establishing a list
    b. Finding dependable players
    c. Dealing with egos
    d. Dealing with subs/cancellations
5. Networking with other contractors
    a. Same city
    b. Different cities
    c. Booking tours

Some may say that these are practical skills that have no place in music school curriculum. Others may balk at adding more coursework to the already frenetic load taken by undergraduates.

But something has to change.

On Hollywood and Baseball

The current music conservatory system is hopelessly broken when it comes to providing music performance students with the skills to be successful in today's employment landscape. A system that has an employment success rate of less than 5% is no success at all. The current system provides a rate of success similar to that of professional actors (and lower than professional athletes), yet most university music programs do not mention these odds or (even worse) brag of effective placement for their graduates to incoming students. Studio teachers also unintentionally feed young students disinformation, relating various success stories regarding their former pupils with pride, conveniently forgetting to mention the dozens (if not hundreds) of former students who never landed any meaningful musical employment after their studies.

If the odds of becoming a full-time orchestra musician are the same as landing on the silver screen and worse than playing professional baseball, fine—just be honest up front. Music conservatories promise one thing and deliver another. Why? Either be honest, or fix the system and equip students with skills relevant to today's employment landscape. No one tells actors that there are these giant organizations in each major city, employing 100 actors each and providing a salary, heath care, vacation time, and a pension. This fiction, however, is sold to music students every day.

If the goal of music school is to provide a purely theoretical knowledge of the subject matter, then music schools should make that emphasis clear to incoming students. In subjects like philosophy or history, there is an implicit understanding that practical, non-circular (i.e. teaching philosophy or history) career paths do not exist. If that is the orientation that music schools wish to adopt for music performance degrees, then they should make this fact very clear to incoming students.

However, if the goal is to provide the music performance student with the skills necessary to be successful, active, fully employed performers of music, then curriculum change is critical.

Programs in which the above practical and logistical elements of a music performance career are thoroughly addressed, including sessions with contractors, officials in both governmental (NEA, local government officials) and labor (AFM, ICSOM, ROPA) organizations and practical training in setting up a private teaching studio, private music school, or an active and viable chamber music organization, would go a long way toward making a music performance degree something that is of benefit to both the degree holder and the musical community at large.

Creating a Scene

If I have one major regret regarding my musical education, it is that I wish I had been taught how to create my own opportunities and build my own diversified musical career in a more logical way. Schools need to address how musicians create a performance organization, organize as a not-for-profit, learn how to book venues, and develop educational programs. Strategies on how to take advantage of grants and programs (both governmental and non-governmental) for securing funding for future projects is of paramount importance.

Learning how to cooperate and collaborate with both musical organizations and artistic organizations outside of music (theater, dance, music stores, art schools and galleries, civic centers) can create exciting new opportunities for interesting projects. When arts organizations work together creatively, they can engage the public in new and exciting ways, helping to strengthen the individual organizations involved in the project.

Educating performers in how to exist as creators of opportunity as well as art has a positive top-down effect on the entire music business as these people graduate and begin their musical careers. More people creating their own performing organizations (educational programs for schools, summer camps, collaborative musical, visual, theatrical, and audiovisual projects, youth orchestra programs, and chamber orchestras) result in more opportunity for other performers.

Do more organizations competing for audience time and interest result in a more thinly-spread audience? The answer is "no" if segments of the population that don't currently engage in classical music activities are targeted. Recent studies indicate that only 3% of the U.S. population would even consider purchasing a ticket for a classical music concert. That leaves 97% of this country's population untapped. Rather than going after that 3%, creative thinkers or entrepreneurs find a way to tap into the huge numbers that aren't currently engaged with classical music at all.

Rather than overwhelming audiences and causing cutthroat competition among arts organizations, increased artistic activity in a community can help rally musical organizations with a collaborative and flexible bent. When managed in an enlightened fashion, arts thrive on each other, causing the community to become a draw for audiences, a "scene" that is much more powerful than the sum of its parts. People go to New York City for the "scenes", taking in the Metropolitan Opera, Broadway shows, the Metropolitan Museum of Art, jazz events, performances at Carnegie Hall, and other events as a total New York City artistic experience. Others check out the Brooklyn Museum of Art, the Knitting Factory, and some smaller clubs, venues, and art galleries. While any of the aforementioned organizations and venues could probably succeed and prosper outside of New York City, being part of the scene strengthens all of them.

In my hometown of Chicago, Illinois, for example, there is a thriving theater scene, with small companies like the Looking Glass Theater and the Neo-Futurarium serving up offerings alongside larger organizations and venues like the Goodman Theatre and the Steppenwolf Theatre. Are these organizations competing for the same eyeballs? Well, yes and no—it depends on how you look at it. What cannot be disputed is that, whether competing or cooperating, these multiple organizations create a Chicago theater scene, a tangible attraction that can draw tourists, folks from the suburbs, and city dwellers of all tastes and income brackets.

In the end, what is most important is not the particular organization but the scene surrounding it. A scene that is highly active is perceived as having vitality. A scene with vitality becomes an attraction for tourists, suburbanites, and city dwellers (i.e. potential audience members). A vital artistic city scene enhances other artistic and cultural aspects of that city. Ideally, a more vibrant and diverse concert scene breeds art galleries, which breed fine restaurants, which breed museums, which breed theatres, which breed more concerts. The reputation and draw of a city therefore improves, thus doing the following: attracting tourism and business to the area; bringing in conventions; encouraging development; and all the other things that most municipalities desire.

Great—so why are the arts either dying or on life support in so many communities?

For most government officials, legislating and budgeting to develop such an artistic scene is like growing orchids in the Arctic—very tricky. Enlightened local leaders may be well aware of the benefits (both economic and cultural) that the arts bring to a community, but setting up the infrastructure for artistic revitalization can be costly and a very hard sell to voters, with no guaranteed return on investment. If the choice is between revitalizing a downtown district in an attempt to foster cultural activity in a city or to sign off on and zone land for a new casino or big box store, the latter choices almost always win out. Casino gaming brings in quick and easy money for a city. So does sprawling commercial development. Benefits from the arts are only realized over time, and in much more intangible ways than the cold hard cash infusion provided by the aforementioned quick and easy methods.

So how do we artists influence change in our own communities and develop our own artistically vibrant scenes? How can we convince municipalities to invest in the long-term high road rather than the quick and dirty low road?

Education and Affecting Change

When was the last time you were in an elementary school general music classroom? Kids at an early age love music just as much as they love sports at an early age. Banging enthusiastically on boomwhackers and Orff xylophones, young kids are musical sponges, open and receptive to all sorts of different styles of music.

Over time, however, many kids move on to other activities, and music becomes, like ballet, a "cultural event" experienced rarely and with great reluctance by the general public. Their perception of relevant music shifts to what is popular on the radio or what exists in soundtracks to movies and television shows. Music for music's sake often falls by the wayside in the developmental process.

Perhaps this transformation from starry-eyed youth to uninterested adult is inevitable. Is it possible for 100% of the population to become art music (classical, jazz, and opera) fans? Probably not. Nothing in this world is loved by 100% of the population, after all. But we can certainly do better than 3% of the population! Increasing the classical music audience size to 6% of the population would double the number of bodies in seats, donors contributing, and people buying albums. Music performers can affect change by making their art a vital part of the lives of all young people. Most orchestras and chamber ensembles already do youth concerts and participate in the schools, but more needs to be done. Many countries (Venezuela is a prime example with its El Sistema program) involve students in orchestra programs, making it a point of national pride. We need to do the same.

The Orchestral Employment System is Vanishing

Orchestral music isn't going anywhere, but its viability in providing a stable income to musicians shrinks with each passing year. Perhaps this is inevitable. After all, this system of full-time orchestra musician employment is a relatively recent development in classical music, having effectively existed for only 50 years. Classical musicians are likely as time passes to assemble their performance careers from many divergent organizations, with only an elite few musicians having a stable, single source of performance income. Music opens new avenues of communication between people, avenues that can never be replicated in print, in words, in visual art, or on celluloid.

In order for music to prosper, we have to be willing to let it evolve, and we keep the art form alive and moving forward by always having art happening all around us. Music majors need to go out and create, invent, innovate! They don't need to be practicing the same stale excerpts for six, seven, or eight hours a day, drilling twenty arbitrary passages from select works of Beethoven and Brahms into the ground, spending their life savings and bankrupting themselves financially, emotionally, creatively, and spiritually for a pie-in-the-sky lie sold to them by the music conservatory system.

The lifestyle and employment prospects for the majority of professional classical musicians will resemble those currently found in jazz, rock, and other musical styles. No jazz musicians expect a full-time job when graduating from music school these days. They are aware of the challenges and pitfalls of their musical landscape, and they take action accordingly, working hard to make connections, develop their own niche in the market, and start their own projects (albums, club dates, tours, and the like). The same can be said for rock musicians.

This is the way things are headed for the majority of classical musicians as well. If hustling to create your own opportunities is a distasteful prospect for you, then you are entering the wrong profession. This is the way classical musicians worked pre-1960, and it is becoming the norm again with each passing year.

What a Waste

In 2006, I took an audition for the Minnesota Orchestra. One hundred fifty other double bassists took this audition. Haggard, antsy, nervous, and twitchy, lugging giant white flight cases out of van cabs and into hotel elevators, these bassists came from all corners of the country on their own dime for a shot at playing in a double bass section. Now, I

Road Warrior Without an Expense Account

love Minneapolis, but if one were to pull a cross-section of people over on the street and ask them what city would be their dream town to live in, Minneapolis would not be likely to make the cut (I grew up a few hours outside of this city, so I speak from personal experience). Cold frozen plains stretch on endlessly for miles in every direction from this northern city, and temperatures routinely hover well below freezing for weeks at a time in the winter.

After the audition, I started to do the math in my head, calculating all of the hours each person spent practicing for this audition, taking lessons, listening to recordings, and all of the out-of-pocket money spent on plane tickets, lodging, car rentals, and the like, then multiplying it all by 150.

Refocusing: Musical Entrepreneurship

Think about it:

Minneapolis Audition Expenses

Activity	Hours or $ Spent x 150	Total
Practicing	200 hrs (20 hours/wk for 10 weeks)	30,000 hrs
Travel & audition	12 hrs	10,800 hrs
Lessons/coaching	$300 (6 coachings at $50/hr)	$45,000
Plane tickets	$450 ($300 ticket + $150 excess baggage)	$67,500
Hotel	$450 ($150/night for downtown Minneapolis)	$67,500
Car rental	$300	$45,000
Food	$200	$30,000

Total: 10,800 hours and $255,000

This one audition took a quarter million dollars straight out of everybody's pocket and over 10,000 collective hours were spent by these ambitious bass players in preparation for this event. Guess how many went home empty-handed?

Cities should hold auditions more often—auditionees are certainly a massive boon to the food, beverage, hotel, and transportation industry!

Think what creative endeavors could have been accomplished by that quarter million dollars and those untold hours! What sort of new projects could have been started, what kind of new opportunities could those 150 musicians have generated with that kind of financial and personal resource expenditure?

We'll never know.

I took that audition. I spent my hundreds of dollars and countless hours preparing. I played for five minutes. I got cut in the first round.

That's fine—I wasn't qualified for the job, or for the other 25 auditions I've unsuccessfully taken in all corners of the country. I just wish that my training had prepared me for this reality.

Now let's see what kind of a toll the audition scene has taken on me—a depressing prospect if ever there was one. Keep in mind that, even though 25 auditions seems like a lot, musicians frequently take twice or even three times as many as this before connecting with full-time employment:

Jason's Cumulative Audition Expenses

Activity	Hours or $ spent x 25	Total
Practicing	200 hrs (20 hrs/wk for 10 weeks)	5000 hrs
Travel & audition	72 hrs x 25	1800 hrs
Lessons/coaching	300 (6 coachings at $50/hr)	$7500
Plane tickets	$450 ($300 ticket + $150 excess baggage)	$11,250
Hotel	$450 ($150/night)	$11,250
Food	$200	$5000

Total: $42,500 and 6800 hours (283 days)

This excludes, of course, the cost of my instruments, bows, and tuition for my two performance degrees, as well as all of the non-audition practicing I have done.

In what other area of life is almost a year of one's life spent traveling and $42,000 out of pocket for a 0% rate of return acceptable?

Art is always evolving. With more artists creating, this helps to develop new opportunities and paths to employment for everyone. Artists collaborating and creating in close proximity helps to establish a "scene," drawing audiences and creating opportunity for everybody.

The audition circuit is a financial vacuum cleaner, sucking musicians dry and leaving them without the means or creative energy to innovate. Ninety five percent of musicians on the audition scene never connect with full-time employment, and the massive expense of both music school and the audition circuit can spell permanent financial ruin for the unsuspecting music performance graduate.

One path is uncertain but artistically compelling, with a bright but still undetermined future. The other path is crystal clear. It just doesn't lead anywhere for the vast majority except the madhouse and the poorhouse.

The choice is yours.

Refocusing: Musical Entrepreneurship

References and Resources:

- Eastman School of Music Orchestral Studies Diploma Program (example of a school adapting to the new employment landscape) http://www.esm.rochester.edu/iml/OSD.html

- University of Illinois Champaign-Urbana (example of a typical four-year undergraduate music performance degree curriculum) http://www.music.uiuc.edu/acadUnderGrad_IP.php

- Chicago College of Performing Arts Orchestral Studies Program (example of a school enacting some progressive curriculum changes, but without adding the business classes like the Eastman program) http://ccpa.roosevelt.edu/music/orch-bm.htm

- International Conference of Symphony and Opera Musicians http://www.icsom.org/

- Regional Orchestra Players' Association: http://www.ropaweb.org/

- Adaptistration – Drew McManus on Orchestra Management http://adaptistration.com

- Polyphonic.org – The Orchestra Musician Forum http://polyphonic.org